What They ?

MW00623898

Cynthia's system simplified my life and brought more clients.
"I've been using Cynthia's Clarity to Cash model for almost a year now and am so impressed with it I had to write a recommendation. I used to struggle to find content and catchy titles for my blogs and other marketing materials, but now it's so easy! Cynthia's system gave me a quick reference guide to creating headlines that grab people's attention. This has simplified my life a great deal and it has brought more clients to my business. Cynthia has a true expertise in content creation and communicating how to do it to people (like me) who aren't marketing experts. I highly recommend working with Cynthia."

Joanie Connell, PhD
Flexible Work Solutions

Cynthia has the ability to help you identify your ideal client/customer.
"Cynthia's expertise and knowledge in regards to marketing and blogging make working with her an exceptional experience. Cynthia has the ability to help identify your ideal client/customer. Her methods guide you to speak your client/customers language with simple marketing content. Using her methods it is easy to create your own library of writing tools for future use. Given the opportunity I would highly recommend Cynthia's one on one program, she is an excellent teacher and mentor. Her Clarity to Cash system works. A gifted speaker as well as teacher, I can't wait to see her book in print with her proven methods. "

Stephanie (York) Sibley
Owner
Charter Oak Preserving Company

Cynthia takes the struggle out of developing a content marketing plan system.
"Cynthia was instrumental for me to move forward and develop a content marketing plan system that is easy to understand, use and attract my ideal client to me. She knows how to work her magic on getting you to know your client's true pain points so that you know exactly how to speak to them. Her methods made it easy for me and now I feel I have tangible headlines, themes and best of all a plan for success! I highly recommend Cynthia for creating your valuable content marketing planning system! She takes all of the struggle out of trying to figure it out."

Luci McMonagle
The Mystic Wealth Creator

She helped me focus my message to clarify what I do for my clients.
"Cynthia's one-on-one workshop enabled me to fully and truly understand who my target audience is for my business and make changes in the way I speak to them. As someone with a technology background, I learned to reword or better articulate my services so that they better capture the attention of potential clients. So they'll feel that my message relates to their current situation. Cynthia helped me focus my message to clarify what I can do and why I'm doing what I do for my desired clients. She helped me create Topic Starters for blogging which tends to be the hardest part in writing about my services and skills."

Frances Naty Go
Web Developer, Goldlilys Media

Cynthia helped me map out my client's greatest needs and desires.
"Cynthia did an incredible job explaining relevant marketing information and offered compelling examples. I left her class with key actions to implement including a format for mapping out my client's greatest needs and desires. I highly recommend Cynthia's services to any business owner needing to reevaluate just who they are marketing to."

Shelley Murasko, CFP, MBA
Wealthspring Financial Planners, LLC

Cynthia gave me insights to improve messaging & attract the right clients.
"Cynthia Trevino's workshop was full of valuable ideas and I left with three great insights about how to improve my messaging to attract the right clients. I highly recommend business owners looking to attract more prospects and grow their pipeline of clients attend Cynthia's workshop."

Laurie Itkin
Financial Advisor, Certified Divorce Financial Analyst

I highly recommend Cynthia's workshops. I learned how to use my client's language.
I've attended two of Cynthia's' workshops. Her advice about how to use my client's language in my marketing is a cornerstone I return to again and again when I explain the benefits of my services to prospects. I highly recommend Cynthia's workshops."

Maggie Frank-Hsu
Digital Marketer for Online Entrepreneurs

Susan,
Be Unstoppable!
Cynthia

She Markets

A Guide for Women Entrepreneurs

Five Simple Steps to Attract More Clients,
Make More Money, and Have More Impact

Cynthia Trevino

Resonnect Publishing

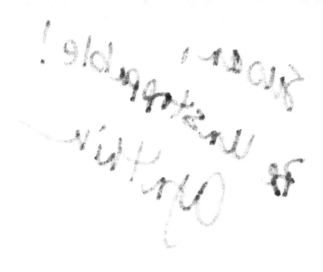

She Markets, A Guide for Women Entrepreneurs: 5 Simple Steps to Attract More Clients, Make More Money, and Have More Impact

Resonnect Publishing

ISBN 978-0-9908252-9-6

To Jim Butz,
my husband, the wind beneath my wings.

Contents

Introduction

Your Marketing Dilemma

You love your work. You thrive on serving. And you pinch yourself every day that you get to be your own boss! You've perfected your ability to zero in on what's keeping your clients from moving forward in life or in business and help them succeed; you are fabulous at what you do. You're the best! If you won the lottery tomorrow, you'd continue doing the work that you're doing today. Nothing makes you happier than helping clients succeed. *But*, if you never had to market your business again, you'd be thrilled.

You struggle to find sane marketing strategies to promote your products and services with intention and purpose. Social media can feel self-promotional to you, in part, because others post photo after photo projecting an image of a wildly successful, picture-perfect life and business. You search for marketing methods that feel authentic and natural to your communication style. At the same time, you want methods that successfully promote your work, your client success stories, and your expertise.

Marketing yourself, your skills, and your business is frustrating for a slew of reasons. For one thing, you're concerned that it makes you seem sleazy at worst and feel overly promotional at best. Right now, you'd rather do anything else than market and promote your business. At networking groups, when it's time to give your 30-second self-introduction, you often want to escape to the restroom until they've passed by your seat.

Every time you're ready to write about your business or explain what you do to a prospective client, your inner 12 year old makes up negative stories. She tells you marketing isn't going to work—it's complicated, you've tried it before, and it would be best to keep doing whatever you're doing—whether it's producing results or not. These wildly false stories intimidate you into thinking you're going to come across as pushy when talking about your business. Experts tell us these old, broken-record thoughts are our inner critics trying to keep us safe. Your inner "mean girl" voice attempts to keep you sealed inside your comfort zone. You end up fearful of testing new client attraction ideas or experimenting with different marketing tactics.

Women entrepreneurs, who continue to allow these old, false, negative stories to affect them, or who are frozen with indecision about what to try next in marketing, end up with empty client pipelines. We need to put an end to this wishful-avoidance thinking and behavior about promoting your business. The reality is, if you're in business, you're in marketing.

Another common reason for feeling discouraged about marketing is it's challenging to find strategies, methods, and tactics that produce the results you're after. The Web is overflowing with loads of get-rich-quick, build-your-e-mail-list-fast marketing and promotional tools, gimmicks, and programs. Most of them don't feel consistent with your purposeful and intentional approach to communicating with potential clients. Your lack of direction coupled with your positive intention around marketing your services and products are likely weighing on your life. In order to have the business results you desire—including the income and freedom you desire—you need a consistent process to attract more clients.

Or, there may be a different set of reasons preventing you from successfully marketing your business. You don't know which client growth strategy to try next because you didn't get great results last time. You haven't found a method that inspires you to be enthusiastic and proactive about marketing your business. You may be procrastinating.

Perhaps, until recently, you haven't needed to be proactive about attracting clients because you've enjoyed a steady stream of referrals. However, things have shifted, referrals are drying up, and you find you must turn your attention to energetically reaching out to—and connecting with—potential clients.

You're Getting Out There

You feel frustrated about the meager outcomes you're getting for the time and effort you spend marketing. You're diligent when it comes to getting the word out about your products and services. You attend networking groups and make sincere connections. You're forming relationships with referral partners. You're writing blogs, recording videos, creating articles, speaking to local groups of your ideal audience, and posting on social media. Good business owner!

But it's doubly frustrating that you're not getting the results you desire and deserve for your disciplined efforts. Despite your sincere efforts, you attract people who aren't your perfect clients. Instead, while struggling to grow your client base, you end up saddled with would-be prospects who are hagglers, tire kickers, or information collectors (people who download e-books, ask questions, take free everything—and never buy or otherwise take action). Your prospects want to pick your brain—often for free. It's exhausting. I know from firsthand experience. At net-working events, despite being present, listening actively, and asking good questions, you're not connecting with enough potential clients. Your "right-fit" people. Your perfect clients. Your tribe.

Vanquish Your Marketing Monster

Does your mind wander to thoughts of what's for dinner or what shows to binge-watch when it's time to compose an e-mail to potential clients? Would you rather clean your entire closet and office in one day than come up with a new blog post or write a fresh, enticing product and services description for your website? Do you stare blankly at the computer screen when it's time to create heart-felt social media updates assuring your potential clients there's hope for their pain? If this is you, you've landed in the right place.

And, you're in wonderful company! Every day I meet purpose-driven women business owners like you. You madly love what you do and yet constantly grapple with how to market your businesses in a manner that's true to who you are. Because you know that in order to have a positive impact on the clients you love serving and reach the income goal you've set for yourself, you must refine your marketing skills, methods, and programs.

Whatever your reasons were for resisting marketing, you've decided it's time for you to finally get a firm handle on the best ways to get the word out about your expertise and promote your business. No more dabbling in social media, no more blogging once or twice a year. No more procrastinating or telling yourself that enough of the clients who need you will (somehow) magically appear at your door, find your website, call your cellphone and say, "I need your services!" This time, you're going to get ahead of this "marketing thing."

Imagine how fantastic you'll feel when you've honed your marketing skills and you're excited about opportunities to start conversations explaining your capabilities with potential clients and referral partners. You will breeze into networking groups, fully prepared to share new possibilities with potential clients. You can organize and implement your marketing content and programs with intention and purpose. Why? Because you'll have a complete, deep knowledge of your ideal client at the center of your marketing and promotions efforts. You'll be able to speak their language. Imagine how confident and certain you'll become after you've created a foundational understanding about the precise type of client who gets the best results from your products and services. After you've developed a deep understanding of your perfect client, you will shape everything you do to promote your business based on them. Your deep understanding of your ideal, perfect client prepares you to speak directly to the clients you want to serve. It allows you to standout from others with a sensitivity to your clients' plight that few entrepreneurs ever take time to cultivate.

Won't it be wonderful to feel more confident about your marketing efforts when you're well-prepared? You'll develop a solid baseline of client insight because you're going to invest time and thought to gain clarity about your perfect client and their situation. This work will be a game changer because you'll no longer be shooting in the dark. After going through this book and applying its exercises, you will have a new framework for creating your marketing messages—headlines, content, and conversations.

Envision how much this rich knowledge and insight will support your efforts to attract more clients. You'll experience less frustration about marketing and promoting your business. Your intention and purpose for starting your business will be well served because you'll be intensely focused on the specific types of clients you want more of. This relentless focus then supports every action you take to increase your income. You'll be more fulfilled when you work with the kinds of clients you love working with, right?

Once you strengthen your marketing skills and improve your results by attracting more of the right kinds of ideal clients, you'll have more freedom. You can stop worrying about how to market your business. Won't that be delightful?

My Instant, Unplanned Path to Being My Own Boss

I love being my own boss today, but my entrepreneurial journey didn't start out this enjoyable. I was enjoying my role as director of marketing for a now-shuttered telecommunications start-up based in Silicon Valley. It became clear that the demand for our once-hot Internet connectivity technology had peaked. Competition was increasing in the already crowded space. But despite mounting rumors, I thought the CEO had time to right the ship. Boy, was I wrong. One morning, as I arrived in Palo Alto on my weekly trip from San Diego, the office was hushed. Everyone's faces instantly told the story. If you've ever been caught up in a massive layoff, you know what I mean. When my boss called me into his office, it was the shortest meeting of my corporate life. After all, he had 60 employees to give the bad news to that day—more than half the company.

Instantly I felt like a total failure. Everything I should have done to prepare for becoming jobless flashed through my mind. My resume wasn't updated. I hadn't cultivated a broad network of contacts. My interviewing skills were rusty. Self-blame washed over me as I berated myself for not preparing for the harsh reality of job hunting over the age of 40.

The next few weeks were devastating because I dwelled deeply on my missteps. I was overweight, out of shape (weekly travel left little time for exercise), and I had no interviewing wardrobe.

My devastation was just beginning. Within a week, I was grateful and thrilled to book two interviews. This was 2001—the telecom industry was in a slump and job openings were scarce. My elation was short lived. In a single week, two male hiring managers gave conflicting reasons for not hiring me. The first one told me I was *too technical* for his position. The second hiring guy said I *wasn't technical enough* for his job opening. Really?

It's difficult, even today, to put into words how deeply this rejection hurt. I was crushed, defeated, and flooded with insecurity and self-doubt. I replayed the interviews in my head. I should have asked the hiring manager more insightful questions. I should have taken engineering classes at night. I should have done more networking.

Driving home on the beautiful San Diego freeway from the last interview, I made an unexpected decision. I was done putting my livelihood in the hands of executives who didn't have a clue where the industry was headed. Kaput! It was unlike me to make crucial decisions in an instant, and yet I did. I was done with corporate life. Instead of looking for a new job, I was going to look for clients for my own business.

For the first two years after becoming an instant entrepreneur my new, small business marketing consulting company went nowhere. I didn't know how to attract the right clients. I didn't know which strategies to try as a business owner. I did everything experts said: print brochures, advertise, put up a website, and network everywhere. I was drowning in advice and not making progress.

I had a constant, nagging feeling that I should know how to market my own business. My unhelpful, critical inner voice ran on a loop, "What's wrong? You led successful corporate marketing campaigns for years. Why can't you market yourself?" I couldn't put my finger on the missing link for how to successfully promote my own business. I dreaded networking because my self-introduction was feeble. And still, I persisted. One night after pulling into the parking lot for an event, I felt physically ill. I couldn't go inside. I was frozen. Sales conversations were a nightmare because prospects said no—or the dreaded, "I'll think about it." I'd hit rock bottom. I'd set myself up for stress and frustration by attracting, enrolling, and working with wrong-fit clients.

I had so much at stake. My husband and I had purchased a new home only three years before. If I couldn't make my business profitable, we risked having to sell our house. Not to mention the humiliation from friends who still held corporate jobs with secure incomes.

I was miserable. My bank account was draining. Things were so bad, I briefly considered getting a job at Barnes & Noble. Then one day, my proverbial "aha" moment arrived. After an excruciatingly painful networking event, I sat down with a glass of pinot noir and replayed the past few years. All of my misdirected conversations came rushing back to me. The fog in my brain lifted. It was clear. I knew what had been missing all along.

I had wasted time talking about topics my potential clients didn't relate to or care about: marketing strategies, marketing plans, buyer personas, campaign concepts, website content, and creating white papers. I could suddenly see that I'd been blathering on like the naïve, inexperienced business owner I was. I used industry jargon and missed opportunities to connect with potential clients.

Unlearning Corporate Marketing

I understand now why my wake-up call didn't come for nearly two years—why it took me so long to see the light that big company marketing was vastly different from marketing myself. I'd mastered heaps of valuable skills during my corporate career like marketing strategy, content writing, researching buyer behavior, and the ability to explain complex products so non-technical folks understood the day-to-day benefits. However, those skills only applied if you're a big brand, rolling out the latest widget.

The cold, hard reality was I had learned zero about how to effectively market myself. I was explaining to entrepreneurs the benefits of marketing strategies, plans, and how wonderful business would be after they became a marketing maven. But this was happening before I clearly understood where they were stuck and what they wanted to accomplish. I finally grasped that spouting benefits is like swimming upstream if you don't first know where your potential clients are stuck.

> **TIP:** When I shifted networking conversations—to focus relentlessly on client outcomes and to speak my clients' language instead of describing my services—it was a game changer. I spoke with increased confidence and felt certain and empowered. I began to enjoy networking and marketing.

In the first four months after changing my focus I enrolled three established, high-end clients. In the first year after my aha moment, I more than doubled my income.

Why? Because projects with right-fit clients lasted for years instead of months or weeks with wrong-fit people. After that, my income grew steadily year over year.

Since then, I've dedicated myself to mastering how to develop marketing strategies that work effectively for solopreneurs and business owners—the marketing that helps you get out of a downturn. I've learned how to guide entrepreneurs like you to build a client-focused foundation that results in more leads, more prospects, more clients, more income, and more impact. After you have this foundation, you're able to attract and work with collaborative clients who are a perfect fit for you, your values, and your business.

Why Should You Listen to Me?

No matter the size of the business, reaching and connecting with the right buyers is a never-ending challenge. I know because I've made thousands of mistakes and acquired an equal number of lessons along the way.

For more than 30 years I've worked with companies big and small to reach customers and clients, fulfill missions, launch dreams, meet targets, and grow income. During my career at Fortune 500's AT&T, I trained sales teams on product rollouts, implemented national advertising campaigns, and analyzed competitors at a time when computers and phones were merging into a single system.

Since co-founding Resonnect Marketing, LLC, in 2001 with my partner and husband, Jim Butz, I've helped clients increase income and achieve their visions by launching books, blogs, products, and services. It's been so rewarding to help clients implement focused, education-based marketing strategies to get from where they were to where they wanted to be. My clients, including start-up founders, professionals, and business owners have become known via social media, attracted clients, achieved visibility that led to awards, and been featured in books.

After all of this, I have much to be grateful for. I'm married to my best friend and business partner. I have the honor of working with visionary entrepreneurs doing valuable work: coaching leaders, creating innovative apps for special needs kids, advancing water rights, developing beautiful and functional websites, guiding start-ups, and more.

My clients inspire me every day. I love volunteering and serve on the board of the San Diego chapter of National Association of Women Business Owners (NAWBO).

My clients are growing their companies by implementing marketing strategies that fit their authentic style, their businesses, and their clients. After our work together, it's rewarding when they express that they feel they can handle marketing because they have a structure to follow and they can think more like their clients think. My clients are confident they can make their content more focused on clients now that they've spent time seeing the world through *their* clients' eyes.

My Promise to You

After you finish this book and its exercises, you will be empowered to communicate to your audience, prospects, and your favorite kinds of clients with confidence and certainty. You already know so much! You possess a golden blend of expertise, experience, and empathy for the clients you serve that no one else has. You may need a tiny tweak, a slight pivot in your "languaging" (words and terms you use frequently), or the emotions you draw on to make deeper connections with potential clients. You may want a new approach to choose topics that your audience of potential clients is most passionate about. Or you may want a process to uncover everything you know about your ideal clients so you can infuse your marketing and messaging with new, deeper insights about who they are. Please join me on this journey to make you the expert in your perfect client.

In Chapter 1 we're going to talk about what's the matter with marketing and why it's a foundational skill for entrepreneurs like you to master. Study after study shows that entrepreneurs, especially women, forget to manage this aspect—the empowered communication that leads to business growth. It's not a slam-dunk topic, practice, or skill for many of us. So, let's tackle it first! Meet me in Chapter 1 to unpack the massive concept of marketing so you can attract the clients you want more of and grow the business of your dreams.

Chapter  1

Your Marketing Quandary

CASE STUDY: JEFF'S NOBLE MISSION

One of my favorite entrepreneurs I've had the privilege of working with was a dynamic start-up founder with a noble mission. Jeff and his wife had a special needs child. As Jeff immersed himself in learning about his son's condition he found that one of the toughest issues for these children is learning social skills. Basic courtesies like how to politely enter a group conversation, make eye contact, and say good morning prove challenging.

Jeff could not find any social-skills learning programs that could help his child and reinforce lessons between therapist visits. Despite not having a technology background, Jeff successfully created an innovative social-skills learning program for special needs children like his own.

He brought me in to help with early marketing when the product was launched. In addition to the typical new product challenges, Jeff faced an unusual level of competition. Apple had recently introduced the iPad and dozens of apps for special needs kids flooded the market. His product was a robust learning program—offering significantly more capabilities than a low-cost app. Jeff's challenge was to set his program apart from the dozens of simple, low cost apps for special needs kids that parents found in Apple's App Store. Jeff had an early concept of the parent who would purchase the program. However, when I explained how we could reach even more of the right parents if we took a deeper dive into getting to know them, Jeff agreed to take time and reexamine his assumptions. We clarified exactly who Jeff's perfect buyer was, because while his game-changing program could potentially help all special needs kids, not every parent was able to invest in it or able to spend the time going through the lessons with his or her child.

The initial marketing, blogging, and social media messages we crafted based on fully developing his ideal parent/buyer began to get traction. We refined our messaging and conversations on social media over a few months. Our diligent work paid off. The product won early customers who loved how it helped their children. Mom bloggers discovered how effective the program was and shared their glowing reviews on social media. Professional therapists at industry events Jeff participated in also raved on social media about how much they loved being able to teach social skills with the aid of the beautiful, interactive video lessons. Additionally, non-profit children's media influencers found the program on social media as did special needs education experts.

The company flourished, expanded with more innovative products, and is going strong today. Jeff's interactive teaching program was a game-changer for special needs children and it led to wild success. From a marketing standpoint, he took three key strategic steps that contributed to his success: 1) as a start-up, he made marketing a priority and brought in an expert to guide strategy development and implementation; 2) he committed resources to an active social media presence including regular blogging which elevated his brand's visibility to both buyers and influencers; 3) he consistently spoke directly to his ideal parent buyer in marketing content and messages even as he refined their profile while learning more about the parents. I was honored to be a small part of this impressive company's early days.

A note about my stories and case studies. Some stories are about men entrepreneurs because as a marketing consultant I worked with both men and women. As an entrepreneur, you may also serve clients who are men.

If You're in Business, You're in Marketing

First: What exactly is marketing? My definition: Effective marketing is sharing short stories with potential clients who don't know you yet about the kinds of results you help people just like them achieve.

Marketing is the fuel for your business engine. It's the nourishment you need for running the pothole-filled marathon that is growing your business, making the income you want, and impacting the people you want to serve. Marketing enables clients who need your expertise, but don't know you yet, to find you. It's how clients discover that you have the answers they've been searching for. Marketing is how you start conversations with potential clients. When you enroll a client (make a sale) you turn a potential client into a paying client. Then your client and you have a relationship, and all good relationships begin with awesome conversations. Don't they?

Your marketing has only one purpose: to start conversations with people who you serve best so you can grow your business and have the life of your dreams. To that end, marketing encompasses every intention you set and action you take to start meaningful conversations with potential clients, by explaining what's possible for them when they work with you. For example, you describe in tangible terms how their business, career, relationship, or life transforms after working with you. Your conversations paint a picture demonstrating how your services, programs, or products help them get unstuck. You talk about how you ease their pain. You tell stories, share anecdotes and information about how you can help them transition from the situation they are mired in today, to their desired destination. It may be a new mindset, skillset, career, relationship, state of health, or physical place they want to be.

Marketing is the set of strategies, tactics, tools, and systems you employ to help reach your ideal, "right-fit" clients. Who are right-fit clients? The folks who show up, are excited to get started, motivated to take action, committed to implement changes you recommend, and who get stellar outcomes from your work! We'll expand much more into how to define your ideal client in Chapter 3.

Marketing helps you make connections with the clients you need to generate the fans, followers, e-mail subscribers, leads, prospects, sales, and income you desire, deserve, and work hard to achieve. It's how you reach, connect with, and move people who don't know you yet into relationships that help you enroll and serve clients and grow your business. Relationships include like-minded people who become leads, prospects, customers, clients, referral partners, collaborators, and/or joint venture partners.

At its basic level that's marketing. You can search online and find thousands of definitions of marketing along with an equal number of methods, techniques, and technologies launching daily. There's a raging river full of shiny new objects to help business owners do better marketing. And YouTube, Facebook, Twitter, Instagram, and up-and-coming social media platforms have all changed the way we make connections and market forever.

TIP: At its core, regardless of which strategies, tactics, systems, or tools you implement, marketing is about reaching, connecting with, and enrolling potential clients who you can provide value to, as paying clients.

Your Marketing Reality

Did you know, according to Capterra Finance in 2016, a whopping 76 percent of entrepreneurs report facing marketing challenges and wish they had more help managing the marketing beast? If this is you, you're in fabulous company.

In our crowded, on-demand digital world, the Internet makes it both easier and harder for you to reach clients. And the Internet makes it tougher for you to educate clients. Why? So much information is available at people's fingertips. There's a tsunami of content. Your clients can pull up articles about your subject on the fly with digital devices and become instant experts. It's your job to let them know you understand their struggles, can help ease their pain, and, as a bona fide expert, can lead them to realize their dreams better than anyone else in your field. You're the expert to educate them on the best way to solve those struggles, ease the pain, and realize those dreams (despite what they may have just read). You must (gently) help them understand that reading a couple of blogs or watching a few videos doesn't (necessarily) make them an expert. Primarily, your marketing goal is to present yourself as the amazing, proven, seasoned expert you are. Your challenge is standing out from the tons of other resources on your topic, by educating your audience of potential clients, using their words and terms, and giving them hope.

Effective marketing is about telling good client success stories well, according to Ann Handley, keynote speaker and author of *Everybody Writes*. It's explaining the amazing results you've helped your clients achieve so potential clients can picture themselves enjoying the same exciting outcomes.

We all do business with people we know, like, and trust. Without a doubt, establishing the know-like-and-trust factor is vital when it comes to attracting potential clients to your business. Marketing is the platform you build—both online and in direct interactions—so you can share your message, talents, and promises with potential clients. It's your vehicle to educate your audience so they begin to know, like, and trust you, your abilities, and your business.

Even for entrepreneurs who studied marketing in college or who were marketing professionals in corporate settings, the reality is the same. No matter how much you study marketing practices, devour books, pour over blogs, view webinars and videos, and digest advice from gurus, until you get out in the trenches and test strategies for your business, you won't know what works effectively for you. Your first step is to actively build your business by trialing multiple marketing and promotions tactics for yourself. Only then do you determine conclusively which strategies and tactics produce the best results and attract the clients you want to work with.

As I've said, there is no magic-pill, one-size-fits-all, easy-button, surefire marketing program. I wish there was! Please be cautious of advice from anyone who tells you there is. You're an entrepreneur with your own one-of-a-kind combination of gifts, skills, knowledge, methods of sharing, and leadership style. Your marketing success formula is based on a slightly different mash-up of tools, strategies, and methods than others in your field. I'm glad you're reading this book so you can enrich your foundational understanding and make informed choices about how to design your unique marketing program.

As good systems do, my Client Clarity to Cash Flow System helps you with, well, clarity. However, you can't get a complete, precise picture of exactly who is your perfect client until you are clear about how you feel about marketing and how you intend to apply its practices to attract your favorite kinds of clients.

I've said marketing is starting deep and meaningful conversations with people who need your expertise so you can explain in hopeful terms what's possible for them when they work with you or when they use your products and services. Your marketing conversations describe in everyday language how their businesses, careers, finances, health, relationships, or lives transform after working with you. And you don't stop there. You explain how your programs and products help them get from where they are stuck to where they want to be. Because everyone who's stuck, in pain, struggling on their own to resolve long-standing problems has a destination. That destination is a point they are dreaming of—a state of mind, physical condition, or success milestone. Today your potential client can only faintly see it in the distance. Your marketing mission is to paint a picture with words, content, images, videos, and conversations that demonstrates how your process helps people just like them arrive at their dream-destination.

You may love, hate, or feel ambivalent about marketing yourself and your business. Love or despise marketing as you will. Without it, your perfect clients—those wonderful people who need your help and would get spectacular results from your work with them, if they only knew you—won't (easily) find you. They won't know that you're the best practitioner, expert, coach, consultant, or trainer to help them. Your ideal clients will miss out on the beauty of your ability to empower them to become the best version of themselves whether that's the best parent, leader, CEO, speaker, teacher, business owner, facilitator, designer, or specific kind of expert. They will miss out on achieving their goals without the support of your guidance, leadership, wisdom, expertise, know-how, and skills. Think of how your clients benefit from your experience as you lead them to solutions they never considered, help ease their pain, and show them how to accomplish big dreams.

Ideal Client, Perfect Client

A note about my use of the terms "ideal client" and "perfect client"—I use them interchangeably. Traditional marketing training uses ideal client to refer to the kind of person/client/customer/user that you want more of in your business. Two other terms marketing experts frequently use to describe ideal client are buyer personas (used by large businesses because they have multiple people to persuade when marketing to reach the actual buyer) and avatar (popularized by Internet marketers).

I like perfect client because it's aspirational. When you're working to grow your business with more clients, shoot for the stars. Make it a moonshot project. Dream big! Describe in detail who your perfect client is and get to know that delightful kind of client who fills you up when you work with them—the exact kind of client you want more of. Why not? You became an entrepreneur, after all, so you can do that thing you love doing and work with people you like.

Define Your Marketing Style

Your marketing style is an approach that works for you and feels natural. Marketing styles are simply methods of connecting with potential clients so you can build relationships. Your marketing style is how you best communicate and connect with potential clients who don't know you yet. It's the manner in which you're most comfortable initiating a conversation, either online or in person.

If you don't master *your* style of marketing your work, it's going to be tough to build a sustainable business. Without marketing, your business you won't start the conversations that lead to relationships that result in the new-client income that enables you to have the freedom to do the things you want to do.

Decide if your current marketing style is true to who you are. Does it feel natural to how you communicate?

For example, yours may be the One-on-One Style. Maybe you're a bit of an introvert and dread large, crowded, noisy networking or industry events. On the other hand, you excel at strategizing individually with referral partners about how to support each other. You enjoy participating in small meetings of two or three like-minded business colleagues. You're great at staying in touch with partners and sharing referrals. You're also successful during individual discovery or strategy sessions with prospective clients and you convert many of them into paying clients.

Or you may have a Words Person Style because you're a brilliant writer. Your words, thoughts, and inspirations for your audience of potential clients leap off the page, smartphone, digital device, or computer screen. Potential clients discover you via your timely e-newsletter, blogs, contributed articles, e-books, books, or white papers. If you've mastered written communications, it may be time for you to focus on in-person communications at in-person events to make it easier to find and connect with more potential clients.

You may be a Networking Maven and flourish at connecting with prospects at business events. Analyze if you're doing enough to transfer your conversation gifts to your online presence. Are you keeping your website and social media profiles up-to-date with your insights and educational marketing messages and content?

Perhaps you thrive on speaking to groups—the larger, the better—so your style is that of a Public Platform Builder. From a marketing standpoint, if you're not already doing so, you want to adopt ways to capture more of your message, power, and expertise into written, published forms of marketing content so that more of your future clients can find you online, via e-mail communications, or in print media.

Whatever your style, be sure you're initiating as many compelling conversations as you need, to make it easy for right-fit potential clients to recognize that you're the one to help them move from point A to point Z. Everyone, from those in pain to those with a moonshot dream they can't quite make happen without assistance, has a point they can see—a destination—of where they want to be when their long nightmare is over. You help them envision that dream more clearly because you explain how you've created a unique set of strategies, tactics, tools, and systems that have helped your clients make moonshot dreams come true or eased their pain. And you've done so time after time.

Client Clarity to Cash Flow System Overview

Mastering the foundational skills of marketing is essential whether you're increasing your income as a company of one or by adding contractors, assistants, freelancers, employees, or some combination of these. Before you can successfully delegate any of the steps I'm teaching you, you'll have far better results by first learning them yourself.

I'm going to teach you the five simple steps to my Client Clarity to Cash Flow System to help you connect with and convert the types of clients you want more of. Because getting clarity is key to setting your intentions, it underlies all aspects of my system.

Step 1 of my Client Clarity to Cash Flow System is firming up your new Magnetic Marketing Mindset. It's about reframing your mindset around marketing yourself and your business. We'll examine how to shore up the way you understand, acknowledge, own, and step into the value you bring to your clients. I become annoyed with my industry because too many marketing trainers do not cover this step.

Step 2 is Meet Your Ideal Client. In this all-important phase, you get clarity about who is your perfect client. An alarming number of women entrepreneurs say they can and want to serve nearly everybody. Then they create marketing content and launch conversations designed to appeal to the masses. This is a giant mistake because it results in messaging that is so generic, mundane, and lacking any specific emotion that it ends up appealing to no one. Not surprisingly, it attracts no one. I'll help you understand the benefits of focusing your strategies, tactics, and efforts on your specific, perfect, ideal client so you can successfully reach and connect with more of them.

In Step 3, you will get a firm handle on Your Clients' Top Pain Points. Here, you uncover and distill your perfect clients' most urgent problems and pressing pain points. Experts advise you to talk about what keeps your clients up at night for good reason. Don't gloss over this step! I'll teach you how to drill down into the nagging, stressful, persistent pain points that keep your clients tossing and turning—and searching for answers.

Step 4 is juicy! You learn how to Speak Your Clients' Language, so you can bring them right to you. You'll discover how to turn your clients' top problems into compelling, irresistible content and conversations. Your content will stop them in their tracks, as they're clicking through their social media feeds and inboxes. Why? Because you'll know them better than anyone else. You're not talking about what *you* think they need. Instead, you discuss topics *they* care about and want to learn about. Avoid sounding like everyone else in your field. Smash through your potential clients' filters and capture their attention by talking like they talk!

Step 5 is Design Your 90-Day Client Connection Plan and it's where you put all your deep work together in a smooth, easy-to-follow road map. This is your personal plan for reaching, connecting with, and enrolling people who don't know you yet. You'll turn them into followers, friends, fans, e-mail subscribers, leads, prospects, and paying clients.

These five steps are all crucial pieces to the beautiful mosaic that is the foundation of your business and your marketing. Are you ready to dive in? Excellent! Meet me in Chapter 2 and we'll explore the importance of Your Magnetic Marketing Mindset.

Chapter 2

Step 1: Your New Magnetic Marketing Mindset	Step 2: Meet Your Ideal Client	Step 3: Get a Handle on Your Clients' Pain Points	Step 4: Speak Your Clients' Language	Step 5: Design Your Client Connection Plan

Your New Magnetic Marketing Mindset to Jump-start Growth and Income

Marketing Mindset Roadblocks

Mindset is the foundation for everything you do to improve your life and grow your business. Your first and most crucial goal in building your magnetic marketing mindset is identifying and overcoming any mental roadblocks you may be clinging to. Many women marketing our own businesses, expertise, and services, struggle with these to one degree or another. Some of us are challenged to boldly use our voice to speak up for the clients we want to serve. Or we're conflicted about speaking up to our perfect clients when we meet them. Your roadblock may be how to sound enthusiastic, without feeling self-promotional, when talking with prospective clients about how you help people just like them achieve results. You may resist asking potential clients to take a small step toward getting to know, like, and trust you. You may be hesitant to invite prospects to your events, join your e-mail list, follow you on social media, or visit your website so they can learn the valuable information you generously share. Or you may be great at all of these but stumble or freeze when it comes to confidently stating your fees during sales conversations.

When you think about marketing yourself—promoting your programs and your business—what comes up for you? Images of aggressive used car salesmen? Loud electronics sales guys pushing big screen TVs before the Super Bowl? How can you think differently about marketing yourself and your business so you won't feel pushy, overly promotional, or sleazy? I have several recommendations.

Let's dump that sleazy auto-salesman stereotype that flashes in your mind when you anticipate promoting your business, shall we? In this chapter, I'll show you how to clear out your mental marketing roadblocks, define your marketing style, and become comfortable discussing the value of your products and services with clients.

Find Your Marketing Style

If you're like me when I became an entrepreneur, finding a way to consistently attract ideal clients and also be comfortably authentic to your style, is as elusive as the pot of gold at the end of the rainbow. As you read in my story, I focused on and talked excessively about my services. I didn't ask the right questions to uncover specific issues and concerns that my potential clients were dealing with.

Mindset roadblocks we come up against, as women marketing ourselves and our businesses, typically fall into one or more of these limiting, restricting beliefs:

1. Marketing is constantly changing, complex, and overwhelming.
2. Whatever you've tried hasn't worked. You don't want to fail again.
3. You're too busy with family, volunteering, and serving current clients to tackle marketing.
4. Fear your marketing won't be *perfect*.
5. You feel salesy, self-promotional, or that you're imposing when marketing your business.
6. You don't know what to try next.
7. You feel like you're repeating the same marketing tactics with no results.

At one time or another, I was guilty of each of these beliefs, feelings, and reactions. I overcame these hamster-wheel habits and I'll show you how to do the same.

Reframe Your Marketing Mindset

Wrapping your head around promoting your work and your business on a daily basis in a fluid, effortless way is your starting point. Here is a realization that was a game changer for me—coming to terms with how I felt about promoting my work. I was reluctant to ask business owners if they needed help with getting more customers or find out about their marketing goals. I felt like it was an imposition. Do you ever feel this way? That you're interrupting or bothering people at networking groups? I sure did. But here's the truth that successful entrepreneurs know in their bones—you're not bothering people. When you meet someone who fits the profile of the kinds of clients you help, you have an *obligation* to let them know who you are and what you do. Especially when you're at a gathering of people who share interests, like Meetup groups, seminars, mixers, networking, or industry gatherings. Yes, an obligation!

The golden insight I want you to gain is this—when you meet people who may be struggling with the kinds of problems you help solve, it's your duty to let them know about your business. Because if you believe they can benefit from your content, your services and products, it is your responsibility to let them know how you help people just like them. Otherwise you're doing both them and yourself a disservice. When you don't speak confidently, frequently, and energetically about the outcomes you help people achieve, both you and your potential clients miss out. Set the intention that you will hone your comfort and confidence level about marketing your business, no matter how far outside of your comfort zone it feels.

Determining exactly how far outside your comfort zone marketing is for you is the next step. We each have our own way of coming to terms with and working through, taking actions from outside our safe cocoon of comfort. Ask yourself, "Is marketing outside of my comfort zone? If so, how far outside? Am I ready to flip this? What baby steps can I take to change this?" Research tells us an overwhelming number of women entrepreneurs, for a myriad of reasons, place promoting their business, and selling their products and services, firmly outside their comfort zone. If this is you, you are not alone by any stretch of the imagination.

Millions of words have been written about why this is so. Experts, psychologists, professors, researchers, and legions of others have tackled the topic. I find in my work that many of the reasons for discomfort about marketing are based on two key factors: 1) lack of certainty about the depth of value you provide clients and 2) diluting your expertise by trying to appeal to everybody with your client-attracting messages.

The lack of certainty, clarity, and confidence about the value your clients gain from working with you is the first one to clear up. Ask yourself, in detail, how much value your clients gain when they work with you. If you aren't clear about the value you bring to the people you serve best—your perfect clients—you'll be challenged to effectively communicate the difference you can make to potential clients. If this is you, consider, one by one, the list of improvements you've made for your clients in the past. Don't gloss over any aspects of how you've helped people change their lives, businesses, health, relationships, or whatever type of services you provide. Are you minimizing your skills, expertise, abilities, and contributions?

Often, as women, we mistakenly assume lots of people can do the things we're expert at—as well as we can. This is simply not true. Because our special genius skills come naturally to us today, we discount how long it took us to master them. Don't lose sight of the myriad of talents and capabilities that make you unique and different. The clients you work with benefit from the sum of all of your gifts. Shortly, I'll give you exercises to help you unpack this foundational element of your marketing mindset.

Marketing Mindset Checklist

As I've said, marketing is showcasing your business, in an it's-all-about-them way, to potential clients who need the results your one-of-a-kind combination of talents and skills make possible but who don't know you yet. It's about making sure the right potential clients know you and your business exist. One of your key mindset steps is wrapping your head around focusing intently on the plight of your potential clients. Put aside your fears and hesitations about self-promoting. Your job is to communicate—in the style that's authentic for you—that you "get" your potential clients. When your all-consuming goal is to convey clearly and completely that you understand their situation, there's little time to dwell on your fears, doubts, or uncertainties.

Marketing Your Business Isn't About You

It's hugely helpful to eliminate any lingering feelings of self-consciousness when reframing your new Magnetic Marketing Mindset because it will be easier to concentrate on educating potential clients when you're marketing. When you think about marketing your business, strive to not focus on your misgivings, reluctance, or uneasiness.

Instead of being anxious about your self-image, keep the clients you want to help top-of-mind. Put aside feelings of anxiety when sharing how your skills have helped former and current clients achieve big solutions and dreams. Remind yourself: you're serving first. Keep a mental picture of the people who desperately need your guidance, coaching, training, and the solution your products and services make possible. Your future clients need your help and leadership! Please don't lose sight of this undeniable fact.

This was my epiphany. It wasn't about me, my skills, or my services. And marketing your business is not about you. It's not about your skills or capabilities. Especially in the beginning, when you're initially forming a relationship with potential clients it's all about them. It's completely about the people you help. You have hard-won experience, knowledge, skills, expertise, and talent. And you have your own unique approach or process for connecting the dots to help them get where they want to go. You have that special genius for solving massive pain points that have plagued your clients, sometimes for years. When you're meeting potential clients, it's not about you. It's about them. Keep the desires and dilemmas of your future clients first in your mind.

TIP: When someone asks, "What does your business do?" don't talk about yourself. Avoid listing your products, services, and skills like a fast-food menu. Instead, share brief stories about clients you've helped. Describe exciting outcomes you've helped clients achieve.

Practice making your initial, getting-acquainted conversations with potential clients all about them. After all, it's the start of a relationship. You want to ask them about the top concerns they want to resolve and dreams they want to accomplish. Find out where they are stuck and where they want to go. Uncover the agonizing problems they want to solve more than anything. Then, paint a picture of how wonderful their life or business will be after working with you or using your products. You're still not talking about your services. You're giving them a peek into what exciting changes open up and are possible for them when they work with you. You're giving prospects a taste of the results you've helped others facing similar issues experience.

Stories You're Telling Yourself

Let's talk about the "old stories" you may be replaying in your mind about feeling salesy. In this case, old stories are negative feelings, preconceptions, or biases about the practice of promoting yourself and your business. Examples of old stories include an inner voice saying you're being pushy when you talk about your business or you're being nosy when you ask people what kinds of problems they're looking to solve. When these old stories pop up in your mind, they can prevent you from being creative and helpful during interactions with potential clients. They can hold you back. Old stories or old fears about marketing or explaining how we help people can limit our growth as marketers. Take it from me, this an all-too-common pitfall for countless women business owners.

These stale stories are another stubborn stumbling block to marketing your business and growing your income that you want to quickly uncover and decisively eliminate. Why? For tons of reasons, beginning with you became your own boss so you can share your talents and gifts, set your own schedule, serve the people you want to help, and take care of your family. And never forget— as you'll hear from me repeatedly because it's vital for you to grasp—there are tens to millions of people who can learn best from you. They're waiting for you. Remain relentlessly focused on your ideal clients whenever you tell yourself the story—whatever yours is—if you're not yet as confident as you'd like to be when promoting your skills, expertise, and your business.

Your story might be similar to those I told myself, "I'm not good enough. I need to learn more, practice more, research more. I don't know as much as others in my field." I recommend you say to that story, "Rubbish!"

Getting a Firm Handle on the Value of Working with You

Acknowledging, internalizing, and understanding the value your products and services bring to clients are crucial foundations for stepping into your value. If you're striving to confidently market yourself and ask clients for fees consistent with the value you provide, you must first be clear about exactly how clients benefit from working with you. Let's explore how you get a rock-solid grasp on your value so you can develop a healthy mindset about promoting and growing your business.

You deserve to be paid what you're worth for a thousand reasons, but primarily because your talent, experience, life lessons, and hard-won expertise help people solve problems. Accomplish goals. Achieve breakthroughs. Your work helps clients become the best version of themselves. Doesn't it?

Don't settle for less money than you know your expertise is worth. You started your business so you can serve the people you're meant to serve. So you can better take care of yourself, your family, and realize your dreams. Besides, you experienced the outdated ways of solving problems in your field, and knew your method was superior. Are you short-changing yourself? Be a mindful observer and notice your attitude and your inner voice. If you find yourself settling, backing off from the pricing you've researched and know you're worth, decide if you want to change that.

As any credible coach or business development expert will tell you, step one to achieving goals is to get clear on what you want to accomplish. Before you can earn your value, you want to get really clear about what is your value. It's vital that you answer this key question for yourself. Let's talk about how to get a handle on knowing your value so you can remind yourself often about how much you bring to the table.

Coaches and leaders who support women entrepreneurs with empowerment lessons constantly repeat this mantra—step into your value. Own your value. How important is it that you understand, acknowledge, and step into your value? It's crucial.

I cannot stress enough how essential it is that you get comfortable with, grounded, and practiced in explaining how clients benefit from working with you or using your products. It's the cornerstone to owning your value. This is true for all business owners. And it's 100 times more important because you're a woman business owner. Sadly, studies show that women entrepreneurs on average pay themselves lower salaries than their male counterparts do. Women are typically hesitant to raise pricing and reluctant to ask for the full value of their products and services. Do you fall into this trap? Never forget, you have a specific combination of skills, talents, and gifts that no one else has. You're your own unique expert, coach, trainer, consultant, creative, leader, professional, mentor, or practitioner. You deserve to earn an income consistent with the improvements you help clients make in their businesses and lives. Right?

Notice if you're resisting setting this intention, "I deserve to be paid for the value I bring clients." Do you take ownership of this aspect of your identity as an entrepreneur? If not, it may be because you haven't yet closely examined the complete value you bring to clients. When they implement your training, follow your recommendations, and solve long-standing problems, their lives improve. Don't they? You see this all the time. Your clients save time and money, and reduce stress and frustration after working with you. They accomplish big dreams or overcome enormous obstacles that were blocking them from better lives. Right? However you help people, it's key for you to revisit how their life is better after they work with you. Call to mind feedback from past clients, envision how their lives improved at multiple levels after they worked with you. Keep these facts close to your heart and on your mind at all times when marketing and promoting your business.

You must be wondering how to easily do this. Don't worry. I have a few writing and thinking activities to help you feel comfortable with understanding and taking firm ownership of the difference you make for clients. Let's begin by taking an inventory of all of your skills, talents, and experiences.

EXERCISE:
WHAT YOU BRING TO THE TABLE

In this exercise, you'll compile four lists that represent the richness of your experiences, skills, and the special genius you possess. It's an easy way to summarize all you have to offer to your clients, including your passions, talents, skills, and life experiences. Use your journal, a separate notebook, or file on your computer to record your lists. Make sure you can easily refer to and update them as needed.

You'll make 4 separate lists:
- Your passions
- Your talents
- Your skills
- Your life experiences

Passions are the things, the people, and the causes you love. These are where you spend time that fulfills you and rejuvenates you. These range from family, friends, and causes you support, to your guilty pleasure pastimes. Include things here like hobbies, volunteering, yoga, reading, bicycling, hiking, creating, cooking, building things, or running.

Your talents are the things that come naturally to you. You may be an accomplished artist, fabulous writer, mesmerizing speaker, scrumptious pastry maker, sought-after project manager, legendary strategist, or memorable storyteller. Remember, these are the things you didn't have to work very hard to learn to do. If you find your talents and passions overlap, include each one in both lists. The purpose of this exercise is to remind yourself of everything you've learned, practiced, and accomplished. It's fine to have duplicates.

Your skills cover things you've taught yourself to do. These can range from blogging, coaching, researching, selling real estate, rock climbing, managing projects, leading people, designing anything, repairing stuff, troubleshooting problems, and more.

Life experiences include the transformational events that have shaped your life and affected how you are able to serve others at your highest capacity. These include events that happened in your childhood or your business career, when you were getting your education, having children, or other events that happened either within or outside of your control. These may be why you can now help others recover from, repair, and resolve major challenges. From your life experiences, you've been able to become stronger and more skilled.

Examine your four lists from time to time. As you redefine your value remind yourself often that you have gifts to share, and people to galvanize, lead, and inspire. Your clients need you! As I've said, there are people who can only learn from you, for whom you're the best expert to help them get from where they are to where they want to go. You owe it to yourself and to future clients to get out there so they can find you. It's sometimes easy to forget just how far you've come and how much you know. If you're not currently earning what you feel you're worth, it can be even easier to lose sight of the value your clients experience when they work with you. Please don't do that.

Another reason it's easy to lose sight of the value you bring is because your particular talent is so darn easy for you today. Your talents, skills, and capabilities are second nature for you now. But don't forget how much effort, time, and heart you poured into becoming as skilled as you are in your field. As women, it's common for us to brush off the fact that not everyone is as competent as we are when it comes to our unique talents and expertise.

You're making lovely progress with your Magnetic Marketing Mindset! Congratulate yourself for taking time to create the affirming inventory of everything you bring to clients, delving into old stories, and overcoming resistance to talking about how you help clients change their lives. You now have one additional, powerful resource you can add to your mindset toolbox.

Commit to a Healthy Marketing Mindset

Promise yourself you will shore up your marketing mindset so you can grow your business. You want to fine-tune your healthy mindset about marketing so you can attract more clients, earn the income you deserve, and make the positive, transformational impact you've set out to make. Once again, be intentional about tapping into your growth mindset when promoting your business. What's a growth mindset?

World-renowned researcher, Carol S. Dweck, PhD, wrote an excellent, understandable book about the difference between a growth mindset and a fixed mindset, *Mindset, The New Psychology of Success, How We Can Learn to Fulfill Our Potential*. Dweck explains that when you put yourself into a growth mindset about, let's say, marketing your business, vast resources open up for you. Over decades of research, she's found that people generally have one of two sets of beliefs about the abilities they were born with.

One set of beliefs is a fixed mindset. People with a fixed mindset believe that their skills, talents, and intelligence are completely determined by what they're born with. They contend that their capabilities are all set in stone. They are convinced they can't improve, learn, or grow in most of their capabilities. They don't believe they can get stronger in a skill, improve their expertise, or enhance their talents.

The second group possesses what Dweck calls a growth mindset. Growth-mindset folks believe that they can always improve, learn more, be inspired to change, and up-level their skills, talents, and capabilities. Growth-mindset people are always extending their abilities. They're constantly enhancing, bettering, and enriching their knowledge and advancing their techniques for getting things done.

Strive for a growth mindset in all areas of your business—you likely already have this belief. You chose to become a business owner and chart your own path. If marketing your business is not high on the list of things you love to do, let's shift that. Extend the growth mindset beliefs you possess for other aspects of your business onto your marketing mindset. Try this affirmation I've adapted from a wonderful yoga teacher I met on a visit to Santa Barbara: "Every day, in every way, I choose to become a better and better marketer."

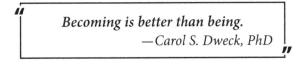

> *Becoming is better than being.*
> —*Carol S. Dweck, PhD*

From a marketing standpoint, when you consistently focus on staying in a growth mindset, you have a desire to learn skills, and adopt beliefs and attitudes to help you become a better marketer. Your desire to learn enables you to embrace challenges, and shed resistance to acquiring and refining your marketing skills. For example, being open to the idea of marketing yourself and tossing aside old-school notions you have about being perceived as pushy or overly self-promotional. As I've said, marketing your business isn't about your needs. It's about the wants, needs, barriers, and situations of the clients you intend to serve. It's about explaining the changes you help them achieve.

Back to your marketing growth mindset: this mindset helps you stand firm and strong if, or when, you encounter setbacks. Even when you have a strong marketing mindset foundation, in the beginning it's not all going to be all champagne and roses. There will be bumps along your road to becoming a master at marketing your products and services. Your growth marketing mindset helps you see that you're on the path to mastering authentic marketing—your way. Also, you don't need to master all marketing, just the specific marketing strategies, tactics, tools, and systems you intentionally choose and implement.

Now we're off to the races! In the next chapter, we dig into step two of my system—getting clarity about who is your perfect, ideal client. Because if you're marketing to everyone, the truth is, you're marketing to no one.

I'll show you how to get clarity about those fabulous, motivated, roll-up-their-sleeves, get-it-done sorts of clients you want to attract to your business.

Chapter 3

Step 1:	Step 2:	Step 3:	Step 4:	Step 5:
Your New Magnetic Marketing Mindset	**Meet Your Ideal Client**	Get a Handle on Your Clients' Pain Points	Speak Your Clients' Language	Design Your Client Connection Plan

Meet Your Ideal Client

How it Pays to Know Your Ideal Client Better Than Anyone

Chad was a wildly successful real estate finance expert with a charismatic personality and gift for storytelling and engaging anyone on any topic. This was especially true when it came to what he did best: finding properties to develop and convert into money-printing machines for his clients. He transformed hard-working, real estate novices, people with 9-to-5 jobs and small businesses, into wealthy investors who regularly quit their day jobs and closed their businesses to do whatever they loved after working with him. For years, he'd been successfully using direct mail, purchasing mailing lists, and advertising in traditional print media to generate leads, prospects, and clients.

Then the Internet got big. So did his competition. Suddenly, his tried-and-true methods for growing his business screeched to an abrupt halt.

When I began working with Chad, I was struck by how well he knew his ideal client. While he didn't use that marketing term, he could describe in minute detail the kind of person who became a successful investor by working with him, following his proven wisdom, and fully implementing his property selection and development techniques.

The barrier I saw was, in addition to direct mail losing its effectiveness and the increasing clout of his competition, Chad had to spend hours, days, even weeks on the phone during a direct mail campaign—screening cold inquires. As good as he was at qualifying, he still had to, well, spend time qualifying. He said, "I hate my phone for a month after a direct letter goes out."

I suggested we talk to his favorite clients for new ideas about generating leads. After a bit of convincing Chad reluctantly agreed. He didn't really think I'd discover anything new, but he was sick of his phone.

It took us no time at all to uncover new ideas. The first of his favorite clients I interviewed told me that there were at least six coworkers at her office who had the same retirement savings dilemma: their savings were too small and they were too close to retirement to build them up. When I asked Chad's charming, chatty client, "What is the best way to introduce your coworkers to Chad?" she said, "Let's have Chad drop by my house one evening. I'll invite my coworkers over and Chad can talk with them about investing with him, like I did."

Boom! Chad did just that. After the first evening "chat with Chad," he had enough new business to carry him for the next four months. It was low-key, no pressure, no PowerPoint, and no selling. Because it was a friendly environment, Chad was simply himself and these like-minded friends of his client self-selected and quickly became prospects and clients. As an added bonus, Chad's original client was a strong, positive influence because she had so much confidence in him and had invited all of them to her house.

The results got even better. Another client we interviewed decided to throw an afternoon barbeque and invited 20 friends with whom Chad could share his investing wisdom. That burgers-and-beer gathering netted seven months' worth of new clients. After that, casual get-togethers with his clients and their friends became a permanent part of Chad's business development efforts.

See how it pays to know your ideal client better than anyone else in your field? You're about to learn how you can do the same.

Who Is Your Perfect Client?

It's been said many times, many ways: Everybody is not your client. You will also hear it from me more than once. What is a perfect, ideal client? Your perfect ideal client is the person who gets the best results from your products, services, and from working with you. These are those wonderful folks who get stellar, fabulous, off-the-charts results from your products, programs, and services. They show up excited to do the work. They share your values. They are motivated, ready, and follow your recommendations. They pay on time, and are respectful of you and others. These are the kinds of clients you want more of because you love working with them. And they love working with you, don't they? The love doesn't stop there. Your perfect clients refer others to you who are just like them. Your next challenge is how to find more of these wonderful humans. It follows that you might think, great, my ideal client is my target market. Are they? Let's explore that.

Avoid the Target Market Trap

My industry asks you to select a target market or a niche market when you become intentional about marketing to grow your business. I detest this method because when you're advised to "identify your target market," like many entrepreneurs, you may end up describing the clients you want to reach in a general, vague way. And because you're not taught the difference, you may settle on an age group and an income level, and consider your work done. For example, a wellness coach might say, "My target market is busy, career women between 40 and 50 who live in Los Angeles." That's a target market, but it's not complete. From that target market description, can you vividly picture one, actual, real woman? No. It's hard to start meaningful conversations with thousands of people. Unless, of course, you're a giant, global soft drink or household name athletic shoe brand with equally giant marketing and advertising budgets.

As I've said, in order to start meaningful conversations with your ideal clients, you want to go deeper and know them better than anyone else in your field does. Let's talk about niche markets. While many marketing experts extoll the value of defining your niche market, it still doesn't give you the advantages of going deeper. Our wellness coach might take a deeper dive and say her niche market is busy career women between 40 and 50 who live in Los Angeles and are overweight and stressed. Now this narrows her market to a more specific group and we begin to see who she wants to reach and serve. Still, we can do better.

I recommend you narrow your niche market even further so you can clearly define, and envision your single, ideal, perfect client. Continue thinking about and narrowing down who exactly is your ideal client, until you can visualize the one person you want to serve. Take a moment and mull this over. If you pause and reflect on exactly who is the kind of person you want to fill your business with, can you picture him or her? If not, let's continue refining your dream client by expanding your description.

The next step is understanding which qualities, attitudes, and mindsets are shared by your perfect clients. Soon I'll give you exercises to help you explore these for yourself. For a moment, to get a clearer understanding of this step, let's return to our wellness coach example. As a purpose-driven business owner, she identifies the qualities, attitudes, and mindsets that define precisely the women in her niche who will take action and invest in her programs. Not every woman who is overweight and stressed is ready to make the changes she needs to make in order to lose weight. Don't you agree? Not every overweight, Los Angeles-based woman in her 40s is motivated to rearrange her schedule, be disciplined, and be committed to do whatever it takes to get the pounds off. Here's the magic. Our wellness coach further characterizes her perfect client as the busy career woman between ages 40 and 50, living in Los Angeles, who is overweight, stressed, and excited to invest in the mentoring of a guided program. This ideal client is committed to following a plan led by an expert. This perfect client is motivated for any number of reasons; she's tried every diet, exercise regimen, and cleanse program out there. Or she wants to feel better, get more done, keep up with her children and grandchildren, or look fabulous at her daughter's wedding or her class reunion. Are you beginning to see how deeply considering a single person who gets the best results from working with you can help you envision them?

To help you picture and drill down to your single, best client, here's a chart I created. It illustrates the layered difference between target market, niche market, and perfect, ideal client.

ATTRACTING YOUR IDEAL CLIENT

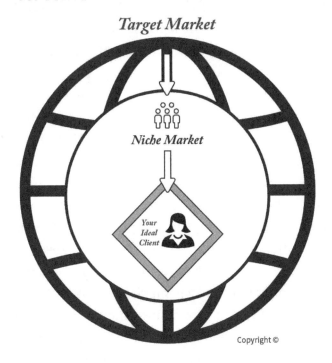

As we go through the next exercises, ask yourself what are the key attributes separating your perfect client from everyone else in your broader target market and niche market.

Why Choosing an Ideal Client Helps Grow Your Business

When I ask business owners to focus on a specific client, it never fails to raise a long list of objections. When you're asked to choose a specific type of client to focus on, your first objection may be, "But I'll miss out on business! My products, services, or programs can benefit lots of different clients. Why should I limit myself to one or a few?" This is a popular question. It feels counterintuitive, but the truth is that focusing on a specific type of client doesn't cause you to miss out.

For those of you over 40 years old, this is the tried-and-true business phenomenon started by the legendary Madison Avenue advertising guys. In the 1960s America's advertising industry was just becoming the behemoth it is today. It was popularized (again) by the AMC series *Mad Men*, which showed how those early pioneers of advertising became wealthy by "meeting your customers in the conversation that's already going on in their head."

If you're younger than 40, think about images and popular quotes on social media that instantly attract the attention of your like-minded friends and are shared hundreds to thousands of times. It's because a brand or a celebrity knows their fans, buyers, and followers so well they can create images and choose words that their audience instantly relates to and loves. These brands are tapping into the worldview, attitudes, and values close to the hearts of their followers.

When you get to better know in-depth the specific kind of client you want to attract, you'll do the same! You'll easily create messaging, stories, articles, emails, social media, advertising, and website content that appeals to them. It makes sense, doesn't it? Because you'll naturally use words, images, and phrases that they relate to. You'll shift your conversation to be more like theirs. You'll begin to talk in a way that compels potential clients to listen. Your ideal clients will relate to your marketing and messaging because you're tapping into their mindset, values, preferences, passions, feelings, frustrations, and more. And this is a good thing when you are crafting marketing content because you'll no longer waste time on topics, problems, longings, and frustrations that aren't priorities for your ideal clients. Their most pressing, urgent concerns will flow naturally into your content. As a result, your content will help you start conversations with potential clients because it will stand out to them. It will grab their attention.

Without an ideal client in mind—getting attention will be tough. What happens when you download your e-mail, check text messages, or open your favorite social media? What happens when you go online shopping or visit your go-to news website? You're greeted with a barrage of messages, ads, offers, links, and more, all screaming for your attention. You've likely adapted your own style of clicking through the Web, social media feeds, and your inbox. You've cleverly learned how to only pay attention to sites, messages, and content that matters to you. You screen out, disregard, delete, and otherwise eliminate the tsunami of messages competing for your attention that *don't* matter to you. Humans are resourceful, aren't we?

Then it's no surprise that your potential clients do the exact same thing. As you step up your marketing activities, you're looking to get e-mails opened, blog posts and videos discovered, consumed, and shared, and some love for your social media posts. To accomplish these feats of client-connection success, you want to emulate the celebrity who knows exactly what's on the minds of her fans. You'll be well-served to teach yourself to speak your ideal clients' language, talk about topics they care about, and share information that matters to them.

And before you can do all of these wonderful things with ease, you must first know your ideal client. And you will!

Choose Your Perfect Client

You Can't Serve Everyone

If you're like most entrepreneurs, you're probably repeating to yourself right now, "But I can serve lots of people! After all, nearly everyone has the problem I help solve." Or you're completely opposed to the idea of narrowing your marketing focus to one specific person or group of people. And while it may be true that you could serve a wide group, as a team of one or a small company, do you want to spread your resources razor thin? Do you want your message to feel so generic that everyone sees himself or herself in it? That's what happens when you try to market to everyone. Your content and conversations risk sounding vanilla, bland, and boring. You'll come across like everyone else in your space. And your potential clients won't be compelled to click, read, watch, follow, or contact you.

I Know My Clients, Why Do I Need a Description?

In much the same way that as a responsible business owner you must prepare an annual business plan and file your taxes, you need to document a profile of your ideal client. Let's talk about why it's crucial for you to get a concrete, detailed description down in writing about the client you serve best. Without a perfect client description, it's like setting out on a road trip or vacation without an itinerary. Marketing with intention is no different. Unless you have unlimited time and budget, you'll benefit from having something similar to a trip route and schedule. How will you know who you're talking to and marketing to without being intentional about who they are exactly? Without spending time to understand exactly who is your person? Your written ideal client description is your North Star. It's your trusted reference for the times you feel stuck about what to do for marketing and promoting your business. It's your touchstone to keep you on track. When you need inspiration, or a creative jump-start to ferret out topics for your blog, video, e-book, downloadable guide, or article—you can pull out your handy, perfect client profile and reignite your imagination. You can refuel your empathy for communicating with your audience.

Once your client profile is documented and you're using it to guide your marketing, you can tweak it, change it drastically, or rip it up and start all over. One thing I know for sure after my 30-plus years in business, you'll learn more as you put your client profile into practice. Marketing, much like life and business, is one, long, Rubik's cube set of experiments. You make informed decisions about who is your ideal client. You then test your assumptions by producing and sharing content, hashing out the issues in your talks to groups, and discussing the pain points in your prospecting conversations. Then you tweak, pivot, and try again until your perfect clients begin to resonate with, and respond to, your message. But the beauty of having a written perfect client profile is that you have a direction from which to start. You make the time to do this work because you care about reaching and serving as many of the people you love working with, and can help, as possible.

I know you're probably thinking that this seems like a lot of work. Bear with me. Here's another reason you want to be as discerning in your selection of clients as possible. Why waste time with tire-kickers who want to pick your brain and aren't serious about investing in your services, or anyone's, for that matter? They are information collectors, whiners, and worse. You've gotten trapped in dead-end conversations and meetings with these slackers, haven't you? These are the kinds of prospects or clients you have to chase down. By focusing your marketing messages and efforts like a laser on ideal clients, you'll also set boundaries for who you are willing to work with. You'll subtly repel and discourage people you don't want to work with. Won't that be a refreshing change of pace?

TIP: Example of (Gently) Repelling People Who Aren't Your Perfect Clients

A web designer introduces herself this way, "I work with growth-oriented entrepreneurs who value customized, professional, one-of-a-kind websites that appeal to their unique audiences." By publishing this statement on her website she'll discourage hagglers who want a quick-and-dirty website. She makes it clear where she positions herself in her industry when she's marketing and networking. She's not the designer to go to for an ordinary, run-of-the-mill website that looks like everyone else's.

If you're going to invest valuable time and resources in marketing your business and attracting clients, let's make sure you connect with as many of your delightful, best-fit humans as possible. After all, that makes it a win-win for you and your clients. They have the tremendous advantages of working with a savvy, caring, purpose-driven expert like you to up-level their lives or companies. And you build your dream business because you work with client after client who fulfills you. Happy dance!

Take Stock of Where You Are

Let's pause now and take stock of the valuable knowledge you have accumulated about your ideal client. You likely already know quite a bit, and we will build on that.

EXERCISE:
CREATE A SNAPSHOT OF YOUR IDEAL CLIENT TODAY

To get started understanding your ideal clients, write down what you know about them today. Answer these questions to get started.

1. How do you describe your target market today?
2. Do you have a clear picture of your favorite client?
3. Does your client description inspire you?
4. Explain how you answer this question from referral partners: Who is a great lead for you?
5. Identify and list the characteristics your past best clients had in common.
6. What qualities, attributes, and values do your past clients share that make you want to work with more clients exactly like them?

We'll expand this snapshot of your ideal client in the upcoming exercises. Doesn't it feel empowering to document and declare who, exactly, is your dream client?

Narrowing Your Perfect Clients' Demographics

Demographics is a thorny topic when it comes to mastering your marketing skills because it can be misused and misleading. While you want to start with the demographics of your perfect clients, too many entrepreneurs stop at these cold, hard statistics about the people they want to serve. Not you! You're going to bypass the stop-at-demographics trap.

Soon you're going to create a demographics list as one step moving you closer to master knowing your perfect, dream client. And then you're going to go much deeper. But first, we'll start with the basics that every business owner uses. Then you will add additional facts and details about your clients that are important to the work you do such as specific technical or other training, major life events, traditions, family responsibilities, depth of business experience, philanthropy level, spirituality, and anything else that is relevant and sets your ideal client apart from others in the broader target market.

Choosing Your 1st Ideal Client

It's time to courageously decide precisely who is the first ideal client you want to market to in your new approach to attracting more clients, making more money, and having more impact. This is essential so you can reach as many of these favorite kinds of clients as possible with your message and your work. This is a single ideal client that you will select and focus on with dogged determination for your marketing efforts. You may remind me, again, that you can serve several kinds of clients and worry that you'll miss out on business.

As I've said, while you can serve many kinds of clients in an excellent manner, for the purposes of this project, you must choose one single, perfect, ideal client. You will take a deep dive into getting to know everything about this wonderful human that will help you attract them. You'll learn how to speak to them so they clearly understand that you have the best products, services, and approaches to solve their urgent problems. You won't miss out on clients. You'll be surprised how effective it is to describe with conviction and enthusiasm the exact types of clients you specialize in helping.

Later, you can return to this exercise and do the work for another ideal client. Please focus on one at a time. This exercise sets the stage for identifying the ideal client you will profile and work on during this project. Are you excited to get started?

EXERCISE:
CHOOSE YOUR 1ST PERFECT CLIENT

STEP 1: List the different programs, services, or products that you offer. This is a summary of the various kinds of work you offer to different types of clients. For example:

1. An executive coach who offers: 1) training classes on communication for professionals and 2) private coaching sessions for C-suite senior managers.
2. A tax professional who: 1) works hourly for small businesses, 2) teaches continuing adult education at community college, and 3) leads an online accounting program for women entrepreneurs.
3. A productivity expert who: 1) promotes her book, 2) gives keynote speeches, and 3) conducts corporate training.

Write down each of the products, services, trainings, workshops, and programs you provide. Include the different methods, formats, and ways that you deliver your products, programs, and services. Yours might include private treatment or healing sessions, VIP days, online or in-person mastermind groups, one-on-one business or health coaching, online self-study courses, leading in-person workshops, retreats, teaching webinars (online), and others.

1. _____

2. _____

3. _____

4. _____

5. _____

STEP 2: Do you help different demographic groups with one product or program? If so, list them. For example:

1. An employee communications program for business owners and for managers who work for a company.
2. A financial planner who serves women and markets to estate planning attorneys for referrals.
3. A relationship coach with programs to help women find their soulmate for both divorced women and never-married women.

List the unique demographic groups that you serve. You will market to these groups using distinctly different, targeted, and specific compelling messages.

1. _____

_____

2. _____

_____

3. _____

_____

4. _____

_____

5. _____

_____

STEP 3: It's time to choose your focus. Be bold! Make two selections. Select one product/service/program and choose one demographic group of clients for your use as you complete the exercises in this book. You can revisit these exercises in the future when you create new programs and are ready to market to, choose, and reach a different set of ideal clients. By putting your attention on one group (for now), you will learn the system more easily. Here are examples to give you ideas for narrowing your focus:

- I choose to focus on: Finding Your Soulmate for Never-Married Women Over 40
- I choose to focus on: Communication Success Skills for High-Growth Financial Services CEOs
- I choose to focus on: Secrets to Securing Your Financial Future for Divorced Women Over 50

It's time for you to make your choice, for now, of just one, single demographic group of clients. Here is an example of how you'd fill out the brief exercise below if you were choosing divorced women over 50 as your group.

> *For the exercises in this book, I will focus on my 90-day post-divorce financial secrets program and get to know my divorced women over 50 group of ideal clients better than anyone else in my field.*

It's your turn to make a choice. Decide which of your client types you will focus on as you read this book. Also decide which of your programs, services, or products you will focus on. Please complete the statement below.

For the exercises in this book, I will focus on my [decide on one of your offerings] _____ product/service/program and get to know my [narrow it down to one] _____ group of ideal clients better than anyone else in my field.

EXERCISE:
GIVE YOUR PERFECT CLIENT A NAME

STEP 4: This is a fun, easy-peasy step. Give your newly chosen ideal client a name. Make it a favorite name, the name of a former wonderful client, or a name to remind you which of your offers they love such as Marathon Mary, Home Loan Larry, Healthy Heather, or Business Owner Oscar. The name is your code word as you work through these exercises and it will help you to connect with your client as you create content. I find using a name for my perfect client helps me envision and talk to them as though they were sitting across the table from me when I create content, blogs, and programs to serve them.

EXERCISE:
FIND A PICTURE OF YOUR PERFECT CLIENT

STEP 5: Here's one more easy step. Choose an image that reminds you of your perfect client. You can pull it from anywhere, because you're not sharing it with anyone. It's a picture you keep close by and refer to when you're creating marketing, messaging, content, and programs for your ideal clients. The image reminds you of who you're talking to. It will help you create from your heart and tune in closely to your perfect clients' desires, viewpoints, and situations.

Now that you've decisively chosen the one, specific, perfect client you'll focus on for this project, we're ready to move to the next phase of painting the complete picture of your ideal client.

Create Your Detailed Perfect Client Profile

You're going to put together a detailed picture of your perfect client as a complete person. You want to get to know them like you know your family. And then go deeper because, to stand out in your field, you want to know your perfect clients better than anyone else in your field and better than they know themselves.

EXERCISE:
BEGIN YOUR PERFECT CLIENT DESCRIPTION

CLIENT PICTURE TASK #1: Jot down the complete list of demographics of your perfect client.

Now let's get into the nitty-gritty of exactly who are your perfect clients. Your first empowering action on your journey is to begin documenting the basics about your perfect, ideal client. In this first task, you will get down every demographic detail that is common to the kinds of clients you most want to work with. It's time to record your list of provable facts about your ideal client (gender, age, industry they work in, job role, income, and number of children).

Age: _____

_____

Gender: _____

_____

Relationship status (involved, married, engaged, divorced, single): _____

_____

Family structure: _____

_____

Children and ages: _____

_____

Culture and language: _____

_____

Education level: _____

_____

Strongest role they self-identify with (single mom, lawyer, advocate, healer): _____

_____

Where they live (urban, rural, suburbs): _____

_____

Household income: _____

_____

Job role/industry: _____

_____

Major life events (tragedies, health issues, deaths): _____

_____

Pitfalls of Relying on Demographic Facts

When entrepreneurs decide to identify their perfect clients, they usually list the age-income-job type demographic facts of their desired clients and call it a day. Even most marketing training starts and ends ideal client work with dry demographics. This old-school training approach drives me crazy. It's a mistake because demographics are the tip of the iceberg when expanding your capacity to study and become deeply acquainted with the complete person your ideal client is. The truth is, when it comes to marketing successfully to reach more of the kinds of clients you want, demographics are merely one sliver of knowledge you'll need.

Instead, you want to get to know them so well that you go beyond the surface reasons to understand how a consumer or businessperson decides to purchase products, programs, and services like yours. Research shows all decisions we humans make are emotional. Then later we rationalize our purchases with, well, rational reasons. In order to uncover the emotional reasons your ideal clients make choices and get stuck, you want to know them like you know your family and you accomplish that by going far deeper than age-income-job facts. Among the dangers of stopping at demographics are that you will miss out on potential clients who are a perfect fit for your work because they don't fall into a specific age group or income category. In fact, they may share the *values* you look for in your perfect clients. Values held by potential clients matter more than facts to you. For example, if you were a health coach you might decide that your perfect client is career women, ages 35 to 45, who want to lose weight. You may learn that a tribe (group) of women over age 45 is highly motivated to get to their goal weight because they've tried everything else working on their own, are feeling stuck, and are ready to purchase a program that provides hand-holding for a 6-month period. They want ongoing support to work through barriers that have stopped them over and over in the past from losing weight. In this case, the revealing attributes for these women are that they are highly motivated, seek group support, respect experts, and admit that they can no longer go it alone. That's a far more precise and purposeful definition than "women over 45 who want to lose weight." Similarly, define your perfect client in a way that gets to the motivated, ready-to-take action, roll-up-their-sleeves people. You want to reach and work with the results-getters. The action-takers. Right?

EXERCISE:
CLIENT PICTURE

TASK #2: Expand your profile and description of your perfect client by adding psychographics, the distinguishing attributes unique to your ideal client.

Attributes, values, and characteristics include things like they're excited to grow their business, they're thrilled about becoming a keynote speaker, they'd rather cook and entertain than do anything else, they are committed to getting healthy no matter what it takes, they are ready to get married, and they are warm, funny and energetic. Base your list of attributes/values on current and former clients who have been wildly successful with your work. Brainstorm and also identify the characteristics they share that make it a joy to work with them, because that's what you want in future clients.

This is where the process becomes fun! It's your chance to begin to see, empathize with, and understand your perfect clients as complete, complex humans. And you can reexamine each demographic fact you've listed. For example, in the case of career moms earning more than $85,000 dollars a year, ask yourself why you've chosen this group. Is it because you think they can afford your products and services? What if they have ample dispos-able income and yet are not *ready* to invest in services or products like yours?

For example, if you were a financial advisor and you had chosen men between the ages of 40 and 65 who are approaching retirement, you would delve deeper. Not all men between the ages of 40 and 65 approach retirement in the same way. Many are not ready to admit planning for retirement is a priority. Not all of them even intend to retire. So, if your reason for choosing men in this age group is that they *should* be planning for retirement, that's a clue that you're not getting into your ideal clients' mindset. Your perfect client may be family men between the ages of 40 and 65 who acknowledge the importance of planning for retirement so they can provide for their children and grandchildren, and spend time doing things they love after retiring. Apply this deeper examination to your ideal client.

For each demographic fact you've listed, ask yourself the reason you chose it. This is how you enrich your deep understanding of who your client is as a person. You'll uncover their attributes, values, worldviews, motivations, passions, beliefs, and priorities. This is how you separate everyone in the broad demographic group (for example, men between the ages of 45 and 60 thinking about retire-ment) from your perfect client (those who are ready to commit to retirement planning).

Now return to your demographics list and add more entries to clarify attributes you've uncovered that further describe your ideal client. These are so-called softer facts butes including values, worldviews, motivations, passions, beliefs, and priorities.

Beliefs: _____

_____

Passions: _____

_____

Priorities: _____

_____

Values (what's most important to them?): _____

_____

Traditions important to them (birthdays, holidays, travel): _____

_____

Personal goals: _____

_____

Professional goals: _____

_____

Aspirations (what are they working to achieve?): ___

_____

Successes (what does "winning" look like for them?):

_____

Fill your list in with other attributes that are germane to your work and clients who have success with your products and services.

TASK #3: Describe traits of the kinds of clients you don't want to work with.

The benefit of this task is to remind yourself of the types of difficult past clients you want to avoid working with in the future. Be decisive about avoiding clients who whine, complain, don't take action, and don't collaborate with you to fix things they say they want help with. When you recall your biggest client successes they're likely people who rolled up their sleeves, implemented your training, took your advice, followed your program, used your product the way they should have, and got stellar results. Right? All because they collaborated with you! When you consider your past difficult clients, they likely weren't profitable for your business because they took too much time, required long discussions while they complained, didn't get good results because they didn't follow your recommendations, they weren't "coachable," you had to chase them down for everything, and more. Don't you agree?

List the attributes of the kinds of clients you want to avoid. Examples include clients who don't pay on time, haggle over everything, waste time, complain frequently, arrive late, are rude to you and others, or are never satisfied with anything you do for them.

List the client attributes you intend to avoid:

1. _____

   _____

2. _____

   _____

3. _____

4. _____

5. _____

6. _____

7. _____

8. _____

9. _____

10. _____

You're the Boss

One note about being clear on the kind of client you *don't* want to attract when marketing: you are the boss. You can always choose whether to work with a client or potential client who contacts you. My recommendation is to build your marketing content, conversations, and messaging so that you pull toward your business the absolute best kind of client you'd like to work with.

As a side benefit, the insights you're learning here about getting ideal client clarity will serve you as you further develop who you are as an entrepreneur. They will help you to develop your personal brand because as you get total clarity about the type of client you want to attract, you'll refine all that you stand for in your business. This, in turn, will make you more magnetic to your ideal clients.

TASK #4: Design your dream client.

Make a list of all the reasons you love working with your favorite clients. Include items like they pay on time, say thank you, are respectful of their own team and yours, are enthusiastic, full of positive energy, and you resonate with their mission.

Describe the qualities of your dream client—the type of person you'd love to have 100 or 1,000 more just like. More possible examples:

- They not only say thank you, they send referrals.
- They are kind, considerate, and friendly.
- They openly share information crucial to a project with you, your team, and theirs.
- They collaborate and treat you like a partner.
- They are committed to serving their customers and valuing their employees.
- They are ethical and you align with their purpose, goals.
- They communicate clearly.

List your ideal, dream client attributes: Get down all the reasons you love working with your favorite clients.

1. _____

2. _____

3. _____

4. _____

5. _____

6. _____

7. _____

8. _____

9. _____

10. _____

TASK #5: Crystallize the reasons your perfect client wants and needs your products, services, or to work with you.

Most marketing training tells you to list your perfect customers' pain points and persistent problems. Once again, my industry fails you if you stop here. It's inadequate. Don't get me wrong, uncovering pain points is crucial and we'll go through them in detail in Chapter 4. However, pain points only get you so far in understanding your people. If you go beyond identifying pain points, you'll create a deeper appreciation for your clients' world. You'll develop a deep empathy for them after you have a complete picture of their experience. Empathy enhances your ability to create products, programs, services, and marketing messages that help you stand out in your field.

Most business owners talk about pain points in marketing content. You, dear reader, are becoming an *expert* in your perfect client and so you explore further. Become familiar with how you imagine their mindset is when they're faced daily with the kinds of problems you help people solve.

In today's accelerated pace of life and business, your clients are juggling a multitude of roles, responsibilities, issues, problems, goals, objectives, too much to do in too little time, dreams, and more. True or not, technology makes us think we can do more, handle more, and get more done. Keep this in mind when considering your ideal clients' world.

Earlier, as you delved into their psychographics (worldview, values, attitudes) you began to better understand what drives them emotionally, inspires them, and motivates them. Essentially, it's their big "why." Their big why is behind the immediate, problem-solving need for your product or service. Is their big why to save for retirement, spend more time with family, start a charity, have more freedom, or travel? Once you get a handle on their motivating drivers, you can have conversations and craft marketing content that expresses, "I understand you. I share your values!"

Write down what you've discovered about your ideal clients' big why:

_____

_____

_____

_____

TASK #6: Clarify how your ideal client affects you.

In this section, you're going to document your feelings about working with ideal clients. These are the positive outcomes you experience that go beyond getting paid for your work. What are the ways it's rewarding for you to work with your ideal clients? Do you feel energized, fulfilled, connected, validated, or something else?

Examples include:

- Excited to see their progress
- Exhilarated at what they're able to accomplish
- Renewed to see your hard work pay off for clients
- Grateful for the opportunity to support others on their journey
- Honored to play a small role in their success
- Fulfilled by helping clients experience personal growth, achieve a life milestone, or solve long-standing problems

---

EXERCISE:
HOW YOU FEEL WHEN WORKING WITH IDEAL CLIENTS

1. How do you feel when you work with them?

_____

_____

_____

_____

2. What is different for you when you work with an ideal client compared to a person who is

challenging, uncooperative, unmotivated, and/ or unresponsive?

_____

_____

_____

_____

Empathy plays a key role when you help clients solve problems whether you work with them one-on-one, in groups, or lead them via online self-study courses. For our purposes, empathy means understanding not only their pain points and problems, but also getting a handle on how they feel about those problems.

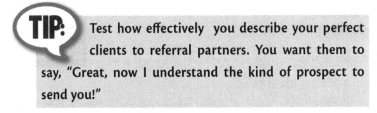

TIP: Test how effectively you describe your perfect clients to referral partners. You want them to say, "Great, now I understand the kind of prospect to send you!"

What If You're Not a Writer?

In your next task, I'm going to ask you to put together a complete, detailed description of who your ideal, perfect client is. You may feel resistant to this step. You may say, "But I'm not a writer. How can I create an entire description of my client?" I understand completely. And you don't have to be a writer for this work to be valuable to you. Here's why. I once worked with Sarah, a lifestyle coach who told me she didn't feel that she was a writer. However, she didn't let that stand in her way. She created a four-page ideal client description. Sarah knew everything she needed to know about her perfect client, who she called "her lady." The four-page ideal client description was all bullets. And it worked beautifully to help Sarah enhance her marketing to attract more of her ideal clients. The format doesn't matter because a perfect client description is your personal tool.

Give yourself the gift of doing this deep work, in any way that works for you. Please keep an open mind and find a method that helps you be present and immerse yourself in who he or she is.

EXERCISE:
CLIENT PICTURE

TASK #7: Assemble the description of the "whole person" who is your ideal client.

In this task, you will put together all the fascinating bits, profound insights, quotes, and exciting discoveries you've made about your perfect, dream client. You'll combine everything you know about them into a chunky, rich, detailed mixture that becomes your perfect client profile. Or, if you prefer, you can write it in story-form or format it like a description. Either way, it's your tool. This document becomes your secret source of inspiration when you get stuck about how to talk to, or create content for, your ideal client. Make it in any style you like. It's your resource, your handbook.

Guidelines for your ideal client description:
- Include all the information you've compiled in these exercises and any previous client profiles you've created.
- It can be as many pages as you need—try for at least one to two pages.
- It doesn't have to be perfect. No one sees this but you and your team.
- Document everything you know and have discovered about them.
- This is a tool you will refer to for inspiration and reminders as you create marketing content.

This is your starting point. Your client description will evolve. As you test ideas about the best, ideal people you want to attract more of you will learn that some assumptions, attributes, and characteristics are accurate. And some are not. You can always tweak this description. It is a resource for you to return to when creating content. It is your touchstone when you prepare for conversations that turn people who don't yet know you into e-mail subscribers, followers, leads, prospects, potential clients, clients, and raving fans. Doesn't that sound like a valuable resource?

Good work! Your ideal client description/story/profile/ guide is the touchstone you will return to again and again. Refer to it when you feel stuck about how to reach, connect, and communicate with the folks you serve best— your ideal clients.

In Chapter 4, we'll go even deeper into getting a handle on how your perfect client *thinks* about their pain points. You're going to know how they talk about their concerns—like no one else in your field. I'll show you how to get a handle on your perfect clients' most pressing problems (from their viewpoint). This is a step far too many business owners skip over. Not you! You'll have a competitive advantage by creating this foundational understanding of the problems they want to solve yesterday. Meet me in the next chapter.

Chapter 4

Step 1:	Step 2:	Step 3:	Step 4:	Step 5:
Your New Magnetic Marketing Mindset	Meet Your Ideal Client	**Get a Handle on Your Clients' Pain Points**	Speak Your Clients' Language	Design Your Client Connection Plan

Get a Firm Handle on Your Clients' Top Pain Points

It Pays to Validate Your Clients' Problems

As reported widely in the business press in 2014 Jessica Mah, cofounder of accounting software startup InDinero, realized that her company was three months away from running out of cash.

While it's not unusual for startup businesses to run into cash flow problems, Jessica was not a first-time entrepreneur. According to the *New York Times,* she'd launched a previous company and, to top it off, she was a celebrated graduate of the well-respected startup company accelerator in Silicon Valley, Y-Combinator. This cash flow crisis was hugely distressing because she'd prided herself on finding gaps in financial services, an industry that she knew well. She'd launched the business by identifying where she could fill unmet needs, grow her company, and repay investors.

But there she was—her products were not cash flow positive. It was clear she needed to retool in order to survive. Sadly, she was forced to lay off her entire team and do some serious soul searching to plot her next steps.

The way Jessica had gotten InDinero up and running in the first place was by understanding what was missing for small business owners from existing accounting software apps. She thought she understood what her customers needed that wasn't offered by the big established players in the online accounting space. Her product was bringing in about $20 per client per month. But now she had to rethink what she *thought* she knew about her customers' needs.

Immerse Yourself in Their World

In the last chapter you defined, profiled, and refined your perfect client from *your* viewpoint. Now let's examine your perfect clients' challenges from *their* viewpoint. In this chapter, I'm going to teach you how to drill down and uncover your clients' urgent problems. Importantly, you're going to learn how to see their world and their problems from their vantage point instead of yours.

I'll give you questions to spur deep thinking about your clients' experiences as they grapple with the kinds of pressing problems that you help solve. You'll have new tools so you can get into your customer's mindset. You'll get in touch with key questions and insights about your ideal clients that set you apart from others. Few business owners look at their clients' world from this perspective. You will get a handle on their most vexing, pressing, and painful problems. Unlike most entrepreneurs, you will become an expert in your ideal client.

See Your Clients' Problems Through Their Eyes

As business owners, we may fall into a dilemma similar to Jessica's. If we've been running our business for some time, we may assume we have a grasp on the exact problems our clients want to solve. Can't we? I want to save you from falling into this trap! Based on the kind of work you do, staying on top of the *most pressing* problems your clients are struggling with is your first goal. Your second goal is to keep current with how they *talk* about their problems. (You'll learn how to talk like your clients talk in Chapter 5.) You'll gain another bonus to mastering an understanding of how your perfect clients experience their pain points. It will become natural to no longer talk about yourself, your skills, experiences, or offers. Instead, you'll share outcomes you've helped other clients, just like them, achieve.

This Is Why You Want to Deeply Understand Clients' Pain

As I've said, too often business owners mistakenly think, "I know what my customers' problems are! My products and services solve them. End of story." It's risky if you don't check in frequently and validate what's tripping up your people. If you don't check your assumptions of where they're getting stuck, you'll miss the keys to communicating and connecting more effortlessly with your clients. If you do not stay tuned into where your clients are, you won't stay abreast of how your market changes. You can miss big opportunities to reach, connect with, enroll, and serve many of your best clients. It's not just marketing mistakes. You can also make the mistake of creating products, programs, and services you think your clients *need,* instead of those they *want.* Set yourself apart from the legions of entrepreneurs who incorrectly assume they know what their market needs.

What does it mean to get a handle on your perfect clients' most urgent problems? It means you view their world, struggles, stresses, and frustrations from a different angle. You step into their experience and imagine how they think and feel about their problems every day. You take off your own shoes as a coach, speaker, expert, consultant, trainer, creator, or practitioner to step into theirs. You momentarily set aside your expert view, analysis, and intellectual understanding of their problems. It's time for you to develop a concrete understanding of how they routinely feel about the problems, pain points, and persistent challenges they're facing.

You also want to assess their level of knowledge about your area of expertise. How much do they know? What have they tried in their quest to educate themselves about solving the concern or issue? How did it work? Where are they stuck? Whatever their degree of skills, experiences, or capabilities are in your area of expertise, they don't know as much as you do. Unlike you, they are not a subject matter expert. Deepen your awareness of where they are coming from in relation to their problems or their dream goals. You essentially determine where they are today, in relation to where they want to be after buying and implementing your products and services, or after working with you. Your benefits of doing this work are profound.

What I love about doing this deep work is that it helps you to become sharper on the best way for you to market and reach your clients. And there's so much more. You end up with a rich understanding of the kinds of clients you want more of, you'll also make smarter decisions about everything you do to attract, nurture, educate, and then turn prospects into paying clients.

Your marketing, content, and messages will land with the people you serve best because they're crafted specifically for them. When you keep your clients' priorities squarely in the center of your mental dashboard you'll create programs, products, and services that help them like no one else. You'll naturally develop education-based marketing content that resonates with them.

Every marketing guru worth his or her salt will tell you one thing you already know: people buy from, hire, and work with people they know, like, and trust. After doing this work, you'll have such a complete understanding of what drives them, you'll more readily establish this golden know, like, and trust factor with right-fit potential clients who have just met you or found you online.

Avoid Feeling Self-Promotional

Here's yet another benefit of doing this work to deeply understand your clients' pain points and how they feel about them. Not from your expert viewpoint, but from the daily viewpoint your clients struggle with. Women entrepreneurs often ask, How do I talk about how I help clients without sounding self-promotional? How do I explain what I do without sounding pushy or salesy? This skill is a big part of your answer.

Once you capture your clients' most urgent problems, you will naturally shift your marketing content and conversations to explaining how you help people like them resolve issues.

Pitfalls of Not Tracking Clients' Urgent Wants

The pitfalls of not taking your clients' urgent wants and needs into consideration when creating and implementing marketing can be devastating to both your client-attraction efforts and your entire business. If you approach marketing with a vanilla/generic description of your ideal client, your messages can be bland. Experts agree that if you're marketing to everyone, you're marketing to no one. You won't be able to apply all of your hard-won expertise and experience, and earn the income you deserve and desire. You won't be able to have the positive affect on those you want to serve. With a generic client description such as "men between the ages of 50 and 60 who are getting ready to retire" or "women over 40 with affluent incomes," you'll have a tougher time reaching and impacting the people you want to help. By investing your mental energy and time to tap into your clients' deepest fears, pains, and frustrations, you avoid the risk of sounding like everybody else in your field.

EXERCISE:
STEP OUT OF YOUR MINDSET AND INTO YOUR CLIENTS'

In this exercise you're going to drill down to your clients' mindset about the issues they need your help with. These questions help you go beyond the actual problems you solve for your clients. Use them to tap into the emotions your clients experience when it comes to tackling the kinds of problems you help them solve.

- How do your ideal clients *feel* about their problems? Or the big goals and desires they want to achieve?
- How do they describe their daily, agonizing frustrations, concerns, pain points, and issues that are caused by their main problems? Main problems are the industry issues you help them fix. For example, your clients may not have the right systems to run their businesses effectively. As a result, they're frustrated by not being able to get away from the office in time to attend their kids' soccer games.

Like all of us, your clients are motivated and inspired to buy based on emotions. We rarely purchase things we *need*. (Unless it's a new set of tires that the mechanic says there's no way around.) We race to scoop up what we *want*.

One of the best ways to view your customers' world from their perspective is to immerse yourself in their pain.

To view the problems you're expert at solving not from your lens, but through your ideal clients' eyes.

Please avoid the common mistake of feeling and acting as though you are your perfect client. I find this too often to be a challenge for purpose-driven business owners: acknowledging that while you may have *been* your perfect client at some point, today you are *not*. You have advanced beyond the issues, pain points, and problems your clients face. That's why you're in the best position to help them! You've gone through their challenges and come out successfully on the other side. You're now uniquely qualified to help them because as a result of your experiences, you've developed the best tools, systems, processes, and tactics to help them fix their problems, ease pain points, or achieve big dream desires.

A Note About Resistance to the Exercises

You may experience resistance to completing the exercises. You may feel overwhelmed and want to skip over them. First, that's normal because you're not used to doing this kind of work. If you've always approached marketing in a general manner, the questions can seem detailed and unnecessary. I promise you it's worth your time and thought because few business owners do this work. You will stand out from others because you've built a foundational understanding of your ideal clients.

No one gets this right the first time, not even me. Here are a few suggestions to manage your resistance: find a trusted business colleague who can be your sounding board and talk the questions and exercises through with him or her; just start writing or typing and get your thoughts out onto paper; when you run out of things to write, put the exercises away for a few days and return to them with a fresh outlook. The exercises will go more smoothly and quickly each time you revisit them. Rest assured, no one sees the exercises but you. The exercises and client descriptions are a living document and they will evolve and improve as you learn more about your ideal clients. Many marketing experts freely admit that they are never completely finished describing their ideal clients, that it's a work-in-progress.

Identify Their Most Urgent Pressing Problems

Take off your expert blinders about your area of specialty. It will help you get out of your own head and further into the mindset of your perfect client. Find a way that works for you to zero in on the devastating problems and golden opportunity priorities of your perfect clients.

Along with the other exercises, this work will serve you well. It is your wellspring for inspiration as you create your own authentic content, messaging, and marketing that acknowledges the deep emotions of your clients.

EXERCISE:
THINK LIKE YOUR CLIENTS THINK

Below are several statements that likely run through your clients' thoughts as they struggle with the kinds of problems you help them resolve. Use these statements to help you grasp their problems, struggles and concerns through their eyes. It's best if you get into a quiet place for this work. Turn off all distractions while thinking through this part.

Record your insights in a journal, notebook, or a fresh document on your computer. You'll be surprised how deeply you can get into their mindset once you begin reflecting on their inner conversations. Revisit this exercise as many times as you need to so you can enrich your connection with their situation. How do your perfect clients fill in these blanks?

- I've got to fix _____
- If I don't find a way to resolve _____, I'll go crazy
- I'm tired of _____
- I'm so frustrated by _____
- This problem of _____ has to stop
- I wish I could _____
- It's time that I finally figured out how to _____
- When I think about _____, I feel _____

Spend time reflecting on the questions in this exercise. To get into the right mindset, review e-mails, texts, and conversations with current and past clients.

Make a succinct list of the problems they want to solve in the next 30 days. This is where your gold is. When you can flesh out the most painful, persistent, and long-lasting problems you will easily uncover what I call their next-30-days problems. You'll have a competitive advantage over other business owners who don't take the time to do so.

Their next-30-days problems are:
- Their most pressing problems, challenges, pain points, and concerns
- Their utmost, top priorities
- The ones they will pay anything to solve

List your clients' next-30-days problems:

1. _____
2. _____
3. _____
4. _____
5. _____
6. _____
7. _____
8. _____
9. _____
10. _____

These problems are the themes you will focus on like a dog with a bone when creating your marketing content and conversations. Much more about that in Chapter 5. Also refer to the section we did in the last chapter, 'why your perfect client needs you,' as you make this list.

After documenting your clients' next-30-days problems you have a creamy-rich resource. In the next chapters I will show you how to use it for creating content they can't click away from, starting meaningful conversations with prospects, and inspiring the design of your next product, program, or service.

I cannot stress this point enough. Staying on top of your customers' biggest, most urgent problem is key to flourishing as a business owner. What you think you know about your customers' problems may not be true.

CHECKLIST:
5 CHARACTERISTICS OF A MOST URGENT PROBLEM

1. **It's a big problem your perfect customer wants to solve.** This is not a small, pesky problem. Too many business owners don't realize they're working to solve small problems. Set your sights moonshot high. Your clients have massive pain points. Your solution is the aspirin, not the (optional) vitamin.

2. **They are mired in this problem.** They are up to their eyeballs in the muck of this issue. It's not simply a common industry problem that experts say they *should* solve.

3. **It is urgent.** They are frantic to find a solution to this daunting, ever-present, boulder-sized problem. It's blocking the path to the rest of their life.

4. **They want to resolve this pain point in the next 30 days.** It's an urgent issue that he or she desperately wants to solve *yesterday*. They are stuck and want to overcome it, or learn how to eradicate it. They're motivated to acquire the skills to work

through it or hire an expert to resolve it once and for all.

5. **It's a problem they will pay *anything* to solve.** Once you demonstrate that you're holding the keys to the kingdom, they're ready to work with you! Once you've shown them you have the answer, they aren't typically going to quibble over the investment to work with you or to buy your product. Their most urgent problems are that pressing.

In our next exercise, you're going to prioritize your clients' most pressing concerns—the ones that are painful and stressful for them every day. What is making them feel stuck? What is standing in their way of moving forward?

EXERCISE:
IDENTIFY THEIR TOP PROBLEMS

Start by making an exhaustive list of every one of your perfect clients' most pressing problems. Refer back to your work from above as a guide. Include every complaint, concern, and issue your clients obsess about. Then, narrow your list to the top five based on your experience with past wildly successful clients. Prioritize your list based on the most urgent pain points, problems, and issues preventing them from being healthy, happy, and successful.

My Perfect Clients' Top 5 Urgent Problems

Top Problem #1. _____

Top Problem #2. _____

Top Problem #3. _____

Top Problem #4. _____

Top Problem #5. _____

Now you have a complete list of the acute, agonizing problems your perfect clients want to solve in the next 30 days to guide your marketing messages, conversations, content, and even creation of products and services. How will you use this valuable list? In each piece of content you create, you'll educate your audience on a small step they can take to move closer to solving their pain. That's another way you build the know-like-trust factor with potential clients.

How Jessica Solved Her Cash Flow Crisis

At the beginning of the problems at InDinero, the company's average revenue per customer was $20 per month. Jessica knew she needed to get a handle on what was missing. She took two strategic steps: 1) she interviewed all of her customers and every other small business owner who would talk to her, "What do you want from an accounting software service?" and 2) she asked herself the moonshot question: what services would InDinero offer if it were a billion-dollar company (like software services giant Salesforce.com)?

She discovered that her customers wanted her company to do more than provide the small online service. Her small business customers told her that they could not afford a full-time tax accountant. They said, "Offer us tax professional services on a part time basis. Do all of the accounting tasks for us." Jessica suddenly realized that InDinero was solving a small problem, while her customers wanted more help. Jessica provided the new services and as a result her average monthly income per customer went from $20 to $400. The next year InDinero was on tap to make $6 million in sales. Mah was so successful at rebuilding her business that she was featured on the cover of *Inc. Magazine* in 2015.

Our next step in the Client Clarity to Cash Flow System helps you develop another powerful tool in your marketing skills toolbox. Join me in Chapter 5 to learn how to delve even deeper into knowing your perfect client like no one else—and communicate your understanding of them with every word of your marketing.

Chapter 5

Step 1:	Step 2:	Step 3:	Step 4:	Step 5:
Your New Magnetic Marketing Mindset	Meet Your Ideal Client	Get a Handle on Your Clients' Pain Points	**Speak Your Clients' Language**	Design Your Client Connection Plan

Speak Your Clients' Language

Jill's Perfect Buyer

Jill was a socially conscious entrepreneur who had developed a luscious, organic skin care line that was flying off the shelf in spas and specialty stores. She sourced ingredients from a developing area in Africa and donated a percentage of sales, prior to being cash flow positive, back to the village. Jill was thrilled about living her dream of building a beauty company and giving back at the same time. She eagerly embraced the concept of "women supporting women."

The problem was that online sales were limping along and nothing she tried moved the needle. When we began working together, her team described their perfect buyers as women between the ages of 18 and 80. That was a problem. She wasn't reaching anyone because she was trying to message and connect with *all* women across four generations with varying lifestyles, priorities, and values. Her website content and blogs were written to appeal to all women from age 18 to 80. You can see why few women were clicking through to her website.

Using my Client Clarity to Cash Flow System, we identified her first priority customer. Jill's perfect buyer was a busy career woman in her 40s who regularly purchased luxury skincare, believed strongly in giving back, and enjoyed discovering new products and online shopping. When Jill got crystal clear on her ideal buyer and revamped the company's messaging, the new content resonated with the right website visitors and online sales grew by more than 30 percent. It was exciting! Jill needed to make the online component of her sales plan to keep the business viable. She was then able to focus on retail partnerships to grow her business and stop worrying about website sales. Let's make sure your business story ends on the uptick like Jill's, shall we?

Your Clients' Language Matters

Are your marketing efforts drowning in a sea of sameness? Do you find that too few of your ideal potential clients respond to your emails, blogs, or videos?

It's time you discovered the words and terms that pull the right kinds of clients to you.

In this chapter, you will learn why it's crucial to be intentional when choosing the precise words, phrases, and language for your headlines, content, and conversations. The truth is when it comes to creating content and conversations that connect with the clients we most want to serve, many of us can fall short. As I've said, marketing is a deep, vast topic. For you, the most important job of marketing when you're looking to get yourself better known and attract more clients is establishing your know-like-trust factor. Because study after study shows that people buy from, hire, and do business with people they know, like, and trust. Your messages create that all-important first impression.

You'll Have Time to Be the Expert

After a reader, follower, or prospect becomes a client, it's appropriate to use your expert or technical language. But, before they know, like, and trust you, strive to help them to quickly realize you understand their situation and see that you grasp their pain. You "get" their struggles and barriers. And you're the expert to shorten their learning curve and get them out of their pain—faster than anybody else.

Let's examine how you can give yourself an edge when composing marketing messages that resonate with your ideal clients.

How to Talk Like Your Clients Talk

If you're wondering how to get a solid handle on the words and terms your perfect clients use with friends, family, and business partners to describe their problems, I've got some recommendations. First, you know more about how your clients talk about their problems than you think you do. You just need to tap into it. You'll pull rich elements from past discussions and feelings clients have shared with you to assemble your client conversation framework. It begins with you imagining your perfect clients' self-talk. Let's explore this.

What Is Client Self-Talk?

What is self-talk? The Mayo Clinic website describes self-talk as the way we talk to ourselves inside our heads. Self-talk can be positive or negative. For our purposes, it's the way your perfect clients describe their problems when they talk to those close to them, or worry about the issue they're struggling with. It's what they say to themselves when they wake at 2:00 a.m. frustrated about a problem. This exercise will walk you through getting out of your expert mind to uncover how your clients think about and describe their problems—in their own words. Scour your memories and recollections of how your current and past clients explained their fears, pain points, and frustrations. When you identify your perfect clients' self-talk, you're getting out of your own expert mindset and envisioning their world from their viewpoint.

How You Benefit from Tapping into Clients' Self-Talk

You'll reap many benefits from tapping into your perfect buyers' self-talk to create marketing messages. Your first reward is that more potential clients will recognize, relate to, and respond to your messages. With potential clients who don't know you yet, you can more quickly build trust because you're using the same language they use to describe problems and desired outcomes instead of your expert-lingo.

If you use highly technical terms in your messaging, content, and business conversations, potential buyers may not recognize that you can help them. If your language is dense, complicated, or filled with acronyms they don't understand, they won't be impressed. They'll simply skip over your content. Or their minds will wander in a face-to-face conversation.

Another beautiful bonus: you will use simpler, more direct words. Picture your content when it's easier to scan and read, and more digestible online. Today, more people search for answers and information on smartphones than on computers. The more your buyers rely on tiny screens, the simpler your language should be. Think about the online ad headlines that attract your attention. They use words and language you're comfortable using, don't they?

As you become comfy-cozy using your perfect clients' everyday language when you're doing client attraction work, more of those who need your help and value your expertise will recognize that you "get" them. They'll say, "Tell me more!" They will understand that you're tuned into their struggles. They'll quickly decide that they want to find out how you can help them. Won't that be a more rewarding way to market your business?

Using Your Clients' Words Helps You Standout

The purpose of your marketing is to make initial connections with more of the kinds of clients you're looking to work with. It's also to stand out from others in a crowded marketplace. Many entrepreneurs sound alike on their websites, in social media, and when introducing themselves in person. You may not realize that, like many of us, you forget to take off your "expert hat" when creating content. We often fall into the common trap of stuffing our content with the industry jargon, words, terms, and buzzwords we've gotten into the habit of using as we became experts. As I've shared, I sure did this in the beginning when I talked endlessly about the importance of marketing campaigns, editorial calendars, and blogging (back when only marketing and Internet geeks even knew what a blog was) among others. Don't make the mistakes I made!

The problem with peppering your messages, content, articles, and networking conversations with technical terms is that potential buyers may not recognize you can help them. They won't imagine themselves being described when they're having conversations with you or consuming your content. Your potential clients are continuously listening for keywords that alert them to their own urgent problems. (Keywords here means their familiar words, phrases, and terms they use to describe their pain points.)

Example of Using Client's Words in Messaging

You want your content to stimulate curiosity and elicit interest from potential clients so they will pay attention to, click on, or listen to the remarkable knowledge you're sharing. To accomplish this curiosity factor in a saturated world of information, help them tune in by consistently using their own, simple, everyday words instead of your expert terms.

Imagine for a moment your business provides software to help CEOs track customer metrics, sales results, and other performance data. You're immersed in your industry terminology. You're accustomed to reading, working with, and using technical software and business terms like tracking, benchmarks, key performance indicators, mobile-responsive software, and more.

Here's how you might fall into the trap of relying on jargon in messaging and an alternative way to phrase it to capture your ideal clients' attention.

> **BUSINESS MESSAGE:** *"We offer mobile-responsive dashboards and reports that help executives deliver better business results."*
> **HOW CLIENT DESCRIBES HER PROBLEM:** *"I'm tired of not getting the data I need to decide how to price our services!"*
> **NEW ATTENTION-GETTING MESSAGE:** *"Are you tired of not getting the data you need to price your services correctly?"*

Finding Your Clients' Words

How do you figure out the everyday words clients use to explain what they're agonizing over? How precisely do they explain the issues they're ready to resolve once and for all? You have plenty of places to look for how they describe problems, pain points, aspirations, and dreams.

Here are a few spots to uncover a cache of your clients' language.

CLIENT SELF-TALK RESOURCE CHECKLIST

- ✓ Pull out e-mails, letters, and text messages from past and current clients describing both their problems and their happy outcomes after working with you.
- ✓ Think through the initial conversations you've had with clients *before* they worked with you and as they started to use your products or programs. How did they describe their problems?
- ✓ Replay past client success stories. Capture their exact words. Put down how they described their results, outcomes, and how their lives are after working with you or using your products.
- ✓ Recreate the emotions they used to explain how wonderful they felt when they finally solved the problem or achieved a big goal after using your product or service.
- ✓ Review testimonials, references, social media comments/reviews, and thank-you messages from your raving fan clients.
- ✓ Recall what referred prospects say, "Jennifer referred me to you because you're the best book-keeper she's found! She said you make the mumbo jumbo about tracking expenses understandable and that's what I need."

Organize your perfect client self-talk according to their specific problems. Imagine what he or she is saying himself or herself as you think about each specific problem. This inner self-talk is likely simple, direct, raw, and basic. It might sound something like:

"I've gotta lose weight before the next class reunion!"

"If I don't get my company's systems under control I'm never going make it to my kid's soccer games."

"I'm nearly 40 and at this rate I'm never going get married."

Let's practice getting into your clients' head, shall we?

> *EXERCISE:*
> ## 15 QUESTIONS TO GET INSIDE YOUR CLIENTS' MINDSET

In this exercise, you're going to record more of the deep reservoir of understanding you've collected about your favorite, most successful clients. And you're going to capture their self-talk. Write at least three to five phrases, responses, and/or sentences for each question below. More is better! As you go through each question, imagine how your perfect client feels or thinks. Recall, in detail, past client conversations so you can begin to think more like they think. Note the actual words, phrases, and expressions they used. Avoid polishing their words with your expert terminology.

Return to, and work through, this exercise multiple times so you can develop a comprehensive library of your perfect clients' words, self-talk, and favorite terms. You'll add more phrases each time.

1. What are they struggling with?

   _____

   _____

2. What are they tired of?

   _____

   _____

3. What are they ready for?

   _____

   _____

4. What are they worried about?

   _____

   _____

5. What frustrates them?

   _____

   _____

6. What are they sick of?

   _____

   _____

7. What do they stress over constantly?

   _____

   _____

8. What are they motivated to fix, solve, or overcome NOW?

   _____

   _____

9. What are they afraid of?

    _____

    _____

10. What are they resisting?

    _____

    _____

11. What are they unconfident about?

    _____

    _____

12. What do they want?

    _____

    _____

13. Who do they want to become?

    _____

    _____

14. What do they want to avoid?

    _____

    _____

15. What do they want to get done?

    _____

    _____

EXERCISE:
CREATE A CLIENT SELF-TALK CHEAT SHEET

After you've ferreted out the delicious, rich, chocolaty words your customers use—compile them into a list. Refresh your memory with this list as you're creating marketing messages and content. Pique their curiosity and stay top-of-mind with potential clients by using, repeating, and echoing the words they're saying to themselves about their problems, difficulties, and dreams.

Your Marketing Headlines Have a Big Job

A picture may be worth a thousand words, but if your audience doesn't resonate with your headline, they won't read your words. They won't open your article, click on your blog, absorb your website services pages, watch your videos, or share your social media posts. If they don't interact with your content, they'll miss out on your exceptional approach to problem solving. If your content headlines don't ignite their curiosity, they're not going to contact you or buy from you.

Your content headlines must accomplish three key tasks according to Ray Edwards, well-known, master copywriter for big brands like Tony Robbins and author of *How to Write Copy That Sells: The Step-By-Step System for More Sales, to More Customers, More Often.*

> "1. Stop the reader in their tracks. They must stop scanning through the copy on the page, and consider the headline.
> 2. Make a promise (either explicitly or implicitly) that interests the reader.
> 3. Evoke enough curiosity to compel them to keep reading..."

And you're amazingly well prepared to write headlines and titles that are meaningful to your perfect clients because in Chapter 4 you cracked the code on what matters to them. Your perfect client work has prepared you to pique their curiosity because you've now identified their biggest pain points. You're miles ahead of most business owners!

This Is Why Your Headlines Must Be Amazing

We are a culture of scanners, not readers. Seminal research by Nielsen Norman Group bears this out: 79 percent of web users scan instead of reading. Your potential clients are constantly quickly skimming like radar, searching for their favorite keywords when online. They're thumbing through their favorite social site feeds every spare moment. They rapidly flip through subject lines in the relentless river of e-mails flooding their inbox on all their beloved digital devices and in the print media they love.

Your content headlines and titles must be mind-blowing because they are your "mini-me's." Think of them as tiny digital carrier pigeons carrying your message. Titles telegraph instantly that you deeply understand where your perfect clients are coming from and that you know their struggles. Your content offers answers, ideas, strategies, and tips they can try. Headlines communicate that you offer them the ticket to freedom from agonizing problems.

Write Headlines Like Tabloids Do

Your job, in the case of writing headlines, is to follow the example of sensational tabloid headlines at grocery and convenience store checkouts. Tabloids scream, "Read me!"

If you're a celebrity watcher or are riveted by the sensational topic of the day, you simply must find out more with headlines like these staring at you:

- What These Celebrities Eat for Lunch Will Shock You
- How to Lose 20 Pounds in 30 Days Without Exercising
- How to Buy a House with No Money Down, No Job, and No Credit
- 25 Easy Meals You Can Make in 15 Minutes Without Cooking

Tabloid writers are well-paid because big brands plunk down equally big dollars to advertise in these publications that fly off the shelves and go viral online. All because tabloid writers understand what fascinates their readers.

You can now compose your own tantalizing titles. And you, dear authentic marketer-entrepreneur, will do so by capturing your clients' actual words. Your headlines will not be sleazy. But like tabloid writers, you will develop attention-grabbing headlines. Yours are based on empathy for your clients' situation. To master this skill, you'll get in touch with how your clients described their pain points. Replay their favorite, constant mantras, words, and phrases they use when describing and reliving their pain and when they are desperately looking for ideas to solve their problems. We're back to education-based marketing.

Reframe Your Content from Your Clients' Viewpoint

Your goal is to create titles and headlines that sum up the burning issues, questions, and problems consuming your clients. That way, you'll be equipped to modify the information and lessons ever so slightly in your article, blog, or video so you speak in a conversational manner. And, you'll communicate how you completely understand their experiences and pain.

A common mistake experts and entrepreneurs make when writing about their subject to capture their audiences' attention is sounding exactly like other experts. It's as though they're talking to peers. Not you! You're creating education-based marketing for your specific, perfect client. That means you're sharing knowledge, tips, and real-world how-to information expressly for potential clients. You're helping them get a handle on solving pain points. Your headlines and content are created in context for where your reader is in terms of his or her knowledge, skills, and awareness of potential solutions. After all, they aren't experts in your field. That's why they need you.

I've harped on this throughout this book because it's essential to your efforts—use your clients' actual words, phrases, and terms. Borrow their straightforward language to describe their pain points, and the outcomes you help them achieve, in your marketing. You'll reach and connect with them more successfully.

Enter as many sentences, phrases, and thoughts as you can in these exercises. You'll use them to create marketing, titles, headlines, and messages. For example:

- E-mail newsletter subject lines
- Article, blog titles
- Headlines on your sales, special offers, and services pages

- Headlines on other website pages
- LinkedIn posts, guest blogs, contributed articles
- Social media posts on any platform
- Titles for videos

Now I'm going to show you how to transform your hard work into a treasure trove of tantalizing titles and head-snapping headlines. We don't want your future clients to miss out on finding you and the incredible help you offer to ease their pain!

Time to Spin Your Tempting Titles

You're going to make good use of the gold mine self-talk list that you created in Chapter 5. It's time to smoothly and skillfully spin titles and headlines out of these golden nuggets of your clients' everyday words.

Your content's purpose is to connect emotionally with readers who can become ideal clients—it's not to sound smart or impressive. (Even though you are!) The tried-and-true what's-in-it-for-me (WIIFM) test applies with every single piece of content you create. And it all starts with the headline—potential clients will scan your headline and think, "What's in it for me if I spend time on this?"

As you complete these exercises, concentrate on constructing titles rich with phrases, basic words, and problem descriptions your people use every day. You will be as happy as four-year old who finds an open cookie bag on the kitchen floor once you've produced your treasure trove of titles. Then I'll show you how to organize them by the top, most pressing problems your perfect clients want to solve in the next 30 days.

Client Self-Talk Building Blocks

This exercise prepares you to build, step by step, topics that will entice your audience to find, follow, and enjoy your content so they will connect with you. After you've assembled your plan, you won't be stuck frantically scrambling for ideas to share with your audience each week. You can pull up your treasure trove of titles—that you've spent time and thought crafting—and inspire yourself to write that blog post, newsletter, or article, or record that video you've promised your audience and yourself.

EXERCISE:
CLIENT SELF-TALK TO TITLES WARM-UP

1. Work from your clients' inner self-talk list you compiled in Chapter 4.
2. Focus on the what-they're-ready-for, struggling-with, and tired-of self-talk phrases you captured.
3. Imagine your potential client is sitting across the table from you. How do you offer him or her hope? How do you explain what's possible?
4. Soon you'll insert what you say to inspire them after these headline introductory statements.
5. Craft 5 to 10 possible phrases for each of the self-talk categories.

Don't edit yourself! In this warm-up exercise, get all of your ideas down. Let your creative juices flow. Think about your poor, muddled clients. Consider how much they're struggling. Stay in the mode of pretending you're sitting next to them. What questions do you ask? How do you help them look ahead to their exciting future possibilities?

- What are they struggling with? What frustrates them? Describe what they're tired of. What are they ready for? Choose the issues, worries, and dreams that you hear most often from clients.

  _____

  _____

  _____

  _____

- What are the sparkling nuggets (actual words and phrases your clients say) you can use in headlines that will compel them to click, consume, and search to discover more about your work? Scribble or type these without editing. You're brainstorming.

  _____

  _____

  _____

  _____

- What concise lesson can you promise them in a headline that will make a small difference in their struggle? What will stop them in their web-surfing tracks to learn more? Switch back to expert-mode for this one. Jot down the quick ways you can help them in an article, blog, or video.

_____

_____

_____

_____

- It's time to give them hope! What do you say to a client, or potential client, sitting across from you at this moment who is pouring out his or her frustrations, to help him or her see that all is not lost? Dig deep and be bold. Get these stirring thoughts and inspiring ideas out of your head and your heart. Transcribe them onto paper so you can use them when attracting clients in the real world.

_____

_____

_____

_____

These are the building blocks for your sparkling, captivating headlines. And then in the body of your article, video, or blog you deliver on the headline's promise by sharing your unique wisdom.

As you begin the next exercises, keep in mind that you'll create many headline combinations to test. Marketing messaging and content—much like life and business— are one giant experiment. Draft 20 to 40 headlines to test on blogs, e-mail subject lines, and social media posts to test and discover which ones resonate best with your potential clients. The way to test headlines is to use them and see which ones your audience responds to. Do 20 to 40 headlines seem like a lot? When I work with my private clients we create as many as 60 to 80 headlines. That way they have a stockpile to try out and determine what their audience of potential clients reacts to best. Once you practice using the templates I'll show you, it will be easier and more fun than it sounds. Pinky swear!

Two Buckets of Headline Styles

Legendary musicians Simon & Garfunkel told us there must be "50 Ways to Leave Your Lover." When it comes to creating headlines that stop your future clients' eyeballs from incessant scrolling through websites and social media, the number of ways to grab attention is way more than 50. Headline creation is its own art and science. Hence the well-compensated tabloid headline writers. As you refine your marketing content skills, you'll adopt other headline types you like and that resonate with your perfect clients. For now, I am going to teach you two delicious, direct, simple, basic, tried-and-true headline formulas—emotional and educational.

Headline Style #1: Emotional Headlines

Style #1 is emotional headlines. These words communicate instantly that you know exactly where your clients are coming from and that you appreciate their situation. You have empathy and know what it's like to be struggling with their issues. Speak to your clients in headlines— like you would if you met them at a social event. Always write and blog in a conversational tone when focused on attracting ideal clients. After all, you are starting a conversation that leads to a client relationship.

EXERCISE:
STARTERS FOR CAPTIVATING EMOTIONAL HEADLINES

Let's unpack your new headline and title-starter formulas. Think of them as pieces of a puzzle you assemble to craft content headlines and titles your perfect clients can't wait to dive into.

EMOTIONAL HEADLINE STEP 1: Choose the starter your audience will relate to from list below.

Emotional Headline/Title Question Starters
- Do you want [blank]?
- Do you worry that [blank]?
- Do you [blank]?
- Do you wish [blank]?
- Do you ever ask yourself [blank]?
- Do you enjoy [blank]?
- Do you need [blank]?
- Do you [blank]?
- Have you thought lately about [blank]?
- Wouldn't you like to [blank]?
- Tired of the same old [blank]?
- Is it time to/for [blank]?
- Is it time you [blank]?
- Are you still [blank]?
- Are you tired of [blank]?

- Are you ready for [blank]?
- Are you sick of [blank]?
- Are you frustrated that [blank]?
- Are you frustrated by [blank]?
- Are you drowning in a sea of [blank]?
- Why should you use [blank] when you can [blank]?

EMOTIONAL HEADLINE STEP 2: Insert the client problem you're solving in this piece of content. Plug in their pain points in their own words. For example, "Is it time you learned how to delegate administrative tasks in your business?"

(BONUS STEP) EMOTIONAL HEADLINE STEP 3: Add the benefit your piece of content provides to readers. For example, "Is it time you learned how to delegate tasks so you can grow your business?" or "Do you wish you could raise your speaker fees and increase your income by 30 percent?"

(FOLLOW UP) EMOTIONAL HEADLINE STEP 4: Test your headlines and titles by using them on all of your content. Track those that result in the most actions from your audience: clicks, e-mail replies, website contact forms, social media shares, video views, and blog comments.

(FOLLOW UP) EMOTIONAL HEADLINE STEP 5: Brainstorm more winners like the ones your audience responds to.

Emotional Headline Examples:

In each part of the emotional headline examples below, I've indicated which of the prior steps it represents. Step 1 is in italics, Step 2 is underlined, and Step 3 is in bold (when it's used).

- *Are you* sick of your website **but don't know where to begin to fix it?**
- *Are you tired of* working around the clock? *Do you need* **expert help to get back time for family?**
- *Do you wish* you could lose those 20 pounds once and for all?
- *Do you worry* your child won't get into college if he doesn't get better at tests?
- *Are you drowning in a sea of* frustration with your business systems?
- *Have you thought lately,* **I'm sick of being in pain every day?**
- *Do you wish* you could feel like your old self again?
- *Is it time* you got control of your debt? **Do you want expert help?**

EXERCISE:
HEADLINE STYLE #2: EDUCATIONAL HEADLINE

Educational headlines can appeal to a broader group of people. They promise your reader that you will "Make me smarter!" Who doesn't want to get smarter? Who doesn't want to learn in a brief three- to nine-minute read things like fresh tips, strategies, steps, or lessons to help us do something better?

Over the next few pages are several headline/title start-ers you can choose from. Create headlines with different starters and see which type your audience likes best. The many advantages of using these templates include:

- Your desperately-seeking-solace readers will leap into your content because it speaks directly to the pain point haunting them,
- You'll use fewer filler words and more of their words, and
- You will teach them one small step on their road to problem solving!

» How to [Solve Something] in [Timeframe]
» How to [Solve Something]

How-to headlines are like honey to bees for your mud-dled potential clients. I love them because they are drop-dead simple to create. Headlines and titles start-ing with "how to" are proven winners in every indus-try. Who doesn't want to learn how to do something or fix something?

Examples:
- *How to Train Your New Puppy in 30 Minutes a Week*
- *How to Get in Shape in 20 Minutes a Day*
- *How to Write a Book in a Weekend*

» How to [Solve Something] for [Specific Client]

Examples:
- *How to Protect Your Small Business from Cyber Attacks for Non-Technical Entrepreneurs*

- *How to Lose Weight for Moms with Kids Home All Summer and Constantly Snacking*
- *How to Start Dating Again After Divorce for Women Over 40*

More starters and examples:

» **Learn How to [Do Something] So You Can [Achieve Goal]**

» **Discover How to [Do Something] So You Can [Achieve Goal]**

- *Learn How to Reduce Your Stress Level So You Can Enjoy Weekends Again*
- *Learn How to Improve Your Team's Collaboration So You Can Launch Products on Time*
- *Discover How to Get More Done So You Can Attend Your Kids' Soccer Games*

» **The Secret to [Blank] or Secrets to [Blank]**

Secrets, formulas, keys, and discoveries intrigue your readers and perfect clients. Try these starters to entice your audience to stop in their tracks, click through, and read your delightful content.

Examples:

- *The Secret to Begin Dating After Divorce for Women Over 40*
- *The Secret to Getting Paid Keynote Speaking Gigs Even If You Aren't Well-Known*
- *The Secret to Accomplishing Monumental Things When You Don't Have a Team*

- *10 Secrets to Financial Security for Single Women Starting New Businesses*
- *5 Secrets to Getting Things Done When You're Stuck and Don't Know What to Try Next*
- *7 Secrets to Closing More Sales with Big Companies in 90 Days or Less*

» Discover the Secret(s) to [Blank]

Examples:

- *Discover the Secret to Public Speaking Without Fear*
- *Discover the Secrets to Launching Your Business While Raising Children*
- *Discover the Top Secret to Happiness After Retirement*

» Discover the Biggest Key to [Blank]

Examples:

- *Discover the Biggest Key to Getting Back Time with Your Family*
- *Discover the Biggest Key to Saving for Retirement Before You Turn 40*
- *Discover the Biggest Key to Social Media for Your Neighborhood Coffee Shop*

» Unlock Your Formula to [Blank]

Examples:

- *Unlock Your Formula to Dominate Your Industry Even If No One Knows You*
- *Unlock Your Formula to Invest in Luxury Real Estate*
- *Unlock Your Formula to Running Your Business While Traveling*

Numbers are super effective to attract attention because they provide the reader with certainty. Experts tell us we like to know what to expect when we click to read an e-mail, post, or article, or view a video. It seems that in addition to liking certainty, we like predictability. A select number of manageable items are appealing to read and learn, right? Simple steps are also fascinating. Who doesn't want simple? Add on dazzling benefits and specific outcomes your ideal clients will jump tall buildings to achieve and make your titles insanely clickable. Do they want time with family, freedom to travel, to find their soulmate, or surefire ways to save for retirement? Add the dream results your clients are longing for.

» (3, 5, 7) Simple Steps to...

Examples:

- *7 Simple Steps to Have a Life Outside Your Business*
- *5 Simple Steps to Delegating Responsibilities in Your Business So You Can Spend Time with Family*
- *3 Simple Steps You Can Follow to Be Financially Secure by Age 65*

» Critical Keys to [Blank]

Examples:

- *Critical Keys to Launching a Side Hustle Business While Still Employed*
- *(3, 5, 7) Critical Keys to Successfully Hiring Your First Employee Even If You Don't Know How to Interview*

- *5 Critical Keys to Planning Your Dream Wedding and Staying Under Budget*

» Master the Art of [Blank]

Examples:
- *Master the Art of Vegan French Cooking*
- *Master the Art of Decorating Your Tiny Apartment on a Tight Budget*
- *Master the Art of Networking to Find a Job When You're Over 40*

» Avoid the Mistake [Blank]

Examples:
- *Avoid 3 Mistakes Entrepreneurs Make When Building Their First Team*
- *Avoid the Top 5 Personal Finance Mistakes Divorced Women Over 40 Make*
- *Avoid the Top Mistake New Entrepreneurs Make When Choosing a Business Structure*

» Learn the Biggest Mistakes that [Blank]

Examples:
- *Learn the 3 Biggest Mistakes That Keep You from Growing Your Business*
- *Learn the 5 Biggest Mistakes That Keep You from Getting Paid Speaking Gigs*

» _____ (Benefit, Goal, Desire) in 30/60/90 Days

Examples:
- *Get in Shape in 60 Days or Less*

- *Train Your Puppy in 30 Days or Less*
- *Master Your Business Finances in 30 Days*

» (3, 5, 7) Ways to [Blank]

Examples:

- *7 Ways to Grow Large, Fragrant, Hardy Roses Your Neighbors Will Envy*
- *5 Ways to Keep Your Business Website Updated Without Spending Hours*
- *3 Ways to Eat Organic Meals When You're Constantly Traveling*

» Clever Tactics to [Blank]

Examples:

- *Clever Tactics to Motivate Your Kids to Do Their Homework Quickly*
- *Clever Tactics to Increase Your Visibility Even If You're New to Your Industry*
- *Clever Tactics to Grow Your E-mail List Using Social Media Without Being Salesy*

» Best-Kept Secret

- *The Best-Kept Secrets of Successful Wellness Entrepreneurs*
- *The Best-Kept Secrets of 6-Figure Keynote Speakers*
- *The Best-Kept Secret of Women CEOs*

» X Excuses That Prevent You from _____

- *5 Excuses That Prevent You from Exercising Regularly*
- *3 Excuses That Prevent You from Meeting New People*

- *17 Excuses That Prevent You from Starting Your Own Business*

» (3, 5, 7) Things to Do When...
- *3 Ways to Amuse Your Kids on Snow Days When You Have Work to Do*
- *5 Steps to Take When You Don't Know Where to Start in Your Job Search After Being Downsized*
- *7 Things to Do When Your Cat Goes Missing*

» Get [Blank] Without Losing [Blank]
Examples:
- *Get Speaking Gigs Without Losing Your Mind*
- *Get Inspired to Start Your Dream Business Without Going Broke*
- *Save for Your Child's College Education Without Skipping Vacations*

You're making exciting progress! You now have a bundle of mouthwatering headlines that will hook your ideal client. All you have to do now is put them into action. Next, we'll assemble your perfect clients' top urgent problems, glittering titles, and true self-talk into a 90-Day Client Connection Plan. Join me in Chapter 6 to top off your fabulous marketing foundation with a structure to help you get your deep, painstaking work and message out so your ideal clients can find you.

Chapter 6

Step 1: Your New Magnetic Marketing Mindset

Step 2: Meet Your Ideal Client

Step 3: Get a Handle on Your Clients' Pain Points

Step 4: Speak Your Clients' Language

Step 5: Design Your Client Connection Plan

Design Your 90-Day Client Connection Plan

Emma Cycles Through a Shift

Emma is one of those stylish, super-smart professional women that I've always admired. Her leadership style is calm, composed, and assured. She's not only a perpetually slim brunette but also in excellent shape. Could it be her ability to bike consistently on top of parenting, marriage, running her business, volunteering, and leading university research projects?

As a successful executive recruiter with hefty credentials, she enjoyed the steady growth of her business. She had carefully constructed, brick-by-brick, a robust referral network.

Then, as often happens in business, things shifted.

Referral sources dried up. Steady clients called less frequently. They say change happens in an instant. It did for Emma. She realized one day that she needed to take proactive action in order to once again attract a steady stream of clients into her business.

Emma's marketing approach, up to that time, had centered on soft marketing—keeping her relationships active by checking in with reliable referral partners and staying connected via networking groups. She suddenly saw clearly that she needed to do something differently. What was working before wasn't going to be enough going forward. She wanted to increase her income so she could have more time for family and travel. While not thrilled about the idea of doing more and different marketing, Emma resolved to find a set of focused marketing actions to bring the consistent flow of prospects and clients she was aiming for.

She found most marketing approaches to be full of hype. She hadn't found a method that was a natural fit with her communications style. She attended one of my workshops and signed up for my Client Clarity to Cash Flow Signature Program.

When we began working together, Emma didn't see herself ever becoming a marketer. Even as an accomplished author and researcher, she found writing to attract clients was a whole different animal. After learning my five-step system, she felt like she could manage this "marketing thing" and get her content out.

She liked learning my 90-Day Client Connection Plan because now she had a structure. Emma used the 90-Day Client Connection Plan to guide her efforts when organizing topics important to her audience, writing and talking in a way so her clients listened, and getting content out for prospective clients to find. That way she could pour enough of her knowledge, wisdom, expertise, and experiences into her web presence and e-mail marketing so potential clients could begin to know, like, and trust her business. She felt confident and certain about how to create marketing that was uniquely "her" after we worked together. After using the Client Clarity to Cash Flow System for a year, Emma reported that she attracted and enrolled more of the clients she loved working with.

Your Journey So Far

Let's take a quick pulse on where you are in your journey to client and marketing clarity. You're nearly at the finish line! You've undertaken the goal of creating a clear picture and profile of your ideal clients so that your marketing messaging, your conversations, and all of your efforts connect with—and attract into—your business the right types of clients. So far, you've painted a clear picture of the person you most want to work with and who is your most profitable client. You've identified her pain points, learned how to get in touch with her specific language, and advanced your skills when creating meaningful headlines to stand out and attract her attention. You're nearly there. Good work! Now, let's talk about the last step, your 90-Day Client Connection Plan.

What Is a 90-Day Client Connection Plan?

Your 90-Day Client Connection Plan is a guide you create to keep track of the type of marketing content you are going to create and publish online (or in print) each week (or month, publishing fresh content weekly is best to be visible) for the next three months. Or the planning period you choose—three months, six months, or 12 months. Your content may be blog posts on your website, social media posts, articles or posts on LinkedIn, podcasts, or videos on any of your channels. Your content may also include articles you contribute to major news and information websites like *Huffington Post,* industry websites, blogs popular with your clients, or print publications specific to your field.

The benefits resulting from you developing a 90-Day Client Connection Plan include gifting yourself the time and space to let your creative educational marketing ideas flourish. Once you have a planning document, you have a place to "park" new ideas that pop into your head. You can continually add meaty inspirations for topics, headlines, or unique twists for articles about your ideal clients' challenges. When clients or prospects ask you new questions, you simply add them to your 90-Day Plan and voila! You have a new source of inspiration when it's time to write, or record new content for your website or social media. Your Plan is a powerful, living, breathing, constantly-updated tool so you can stay on track with sharing what you want to contribute to your potential clients' world. And you're making it easier for your next perfect client to find you because of your fascinating, amazing, steady stream of marketing content.

You're now ready to take everything you've prepared and organize it into your fabulous 90-Day Client Connection Plan. Your plan will help you carry your hard work out into the world so you can find and connect with more wonderful future clients. It will be your guidepost and go-to reference as you add business building tasks and activities to your calendar. Then it's up to you to implement your Plan. Nothing happens to attract more clients into your business until you take action—knowing your perfect clients better than anyone, learning to speak their language, creating fabulous content, and getting it out there regularly.

Your 90-Day Client Connection Plan eliminates the dreaded dilemma of asking yourself, "What should I do for marketing now?" Instead, you can spend your valuable time creating marketing, messaging, and content that skillfully and elegantly shares stories about the kinds of people you help and the ways you help them. Are you ready to create your Plan?

Gather Up Your Perfect Client Tools

In this step, you will pull together all the work you've done up to now and wrap it into a luscious, practical package of tools to make your life easier each time you create marketing content. You've dug deep to create a library of words and phrases your unique, ideal clients use regularly. You've prepared a rich, long list of attention-grabbing headlines.

CHECKLIST

Now organize all this thorough background work you've completed into a binder or separate file on your computer, if you haven't already done so.

- ✓ Your perfect client description
- ✓ A complete list of your clients' most urgent pain points
- ✓ Your client language list packed with words, phrases, and terms your perfect clients commonly use when describing pain points and problems
- ✓ Your clients' frequently asked questions (FAQ) and should ask questions (SAQ)
- ✓ Your client success words list: how they describe their outcomes after working with you—unedited, unpolished, in their own words
- ✓ Your treasure trove of headlines speaking to your ideal clients' specific pain points

---

The steps that follow show you how to choose pain point themes and organize the topics you create educational content about. You want as much educational content for your blog, webpages, LinkedIn, other social media accounts, videos, contributed articles to news and industry publications as you can pull together. It's all so you can better attract, connect with, and transform fans, readers, and followers into e-mail list subscribers and paying clients.

90-DAY PLAN STEP #1: Decide how often you intend to publish fresh content. Do you want to create new content monthly, weekly, or more often? Experts say once each week is best; select the frequency that fits your audience, time, and resources. Some entrepreneurs find that their potential client audience is fine with monthly new posts while others prefer twice a week. If you have a team, you may post more often. Whichever frequency you choose, be consistent.

90-DAY PLAN STEP #2: Select a pain point theme for each week. A pain point theme is one of your ideal clients' high-level pain points, urgent problems, or dreams you identified in Chapter 4.

Alternate themes each time you create content. When you reach the end of your themes, simply recycle; go back to the beginning and create different content for the same themes. That's why you created so many variations of headlines for each urgent pain point.

Don't worry about repeats or duplication. Each piece of content on the same theme will vary slightly thanks to your robust list of headlines. Your audience will rarely (if ever) consume all of your content each week because they discover your website, blog, or social media profile at different times. Be sure to alternate content on different client pain point topics regularly. That way, no matter which of the top urgent pain points is on your clients' mind when they find your article, video, blog, website, or social media posts, you have a good chance of sparking their interest with a range of headlines.

Example: Pain Point Theme
Pain point theme examples for a relationship coach who serves divorced women over 40 looking for their soulmate might be:

   1) How to meet men without going to bars
   2) Managing the dreaded blind date setup
   3) How to talk to a man you're dating so you can determine if he's compatible for you

---

This coach can create multiple pieces of content to explain and educate her audience of future clients on different aspects of each pain point theme.

   In the future, if you add additional perfect clients to your business, choose themes for each of your perfect client profiles and alternate content each time you publish. For example, publish content for perfect client #1 one week, perfect client #2 the next week, and so forth. Or if you publish more frequently than once a week, find a rotation that works for you. You want each of your perfect client types to discover recent content that talks about their priorities when they visit your website or your social profiles.

90-DAY PLAN STEP #3: Pick one of your sparkling headlines for each pain point theme. This is the work I taught you in Chapter 5. Aren't you glad you crafted several captivating headlines focused on your perfect clients' priorities? Now you can select one, paste it into your Plan, and when it's time to write an article, blog, or video script, you don't have to stare at a blank screen wondering what to talk about. Rotate themes until you have used all of your headlines. Then create a new set of headlines under each of your themes.

Here is how you put together Steps #2 and #3.

The following are examples if you plan to create educational marketing content weekly.

This example is how a small business bookkeeper accounting business organizes her content:

PAIN POINT THEME WEEK 1: *How to manage your business finances and expenses when you're not an accountant*
> HEADLINE: 5 *Signs It's Time You Got Expert Help to Track Business Expenses*

PAIN POINT THEME WEEK 2: *Finding time to keep up with your business expenses*
> HEADLINE: *Are You Drowning in a Sea of Random Receipts, Unfiled Reports, and Outdated Bookkeeping Software?*

PAIN POINT THEME WEEK 3: *I don't know how to choose and work with an accounting professional for my small business*
> HEADLINE: 5 *Things to Remember When Choosing an Accountant for Your Business*

PAIN POINT THEME WEEK 4: *I don't know how to track and manage cash flow for my new business*
> HEADLINE: *How to Manage Your New Small Business Cash Flow Like a Boss*

PAIN POINT THEME WEEK 5: *Recycle pain point themes by returning to week 1 theme: How to manage your business finances and expenses when you're not an accountant.*
> HEADLINE: 7 *Secrets to Choosing an Expert to Help You Manage Your Finances When You're Growing Your Business*

Continue each week as above.

90-DAY PLAN STEP #4: Assemble your Plan into a document or spreadsheet. Insert your pain point themes and headlines. Set up the document, or spreadsheet according to the timeframes you've decided on to publish and promote your content. By promote, I mean encourage people to visit your website by sharing links back to your blog on your social media channels. This way you can invite web visitors to sign up for your mailing list to stay updated when you publish new articles.

You've Accomplished So Much!

I am thrilled about the progress you've made. Too few experts and business owners invest in this deep work. You have a distinct competitive advantage now. You know your ideal client better than anyone else in your space. Now you know how to use your perfect clients' words, and come from their viewpoint so you can create content tailored to their world and connect with more of them.

Meet me in the last chapter and I'll share ways to empower yourself to stay on track of creating content and conversations for your ideal clients so you can increase your business income and have more fun.

Chapter 7

Map Out Your Moonshot Marketing Moves

Take Care of Your Business

Congratulations! You've done it! You now know your ideal client better than anyone else in your field. You've given yourself the gift of a deep understanding of what frustrates them, what they're tired of, and (best of all) what they're ready for. You're prepared to attract your ideal clients' attention online with headlines written just for them, explain who you help in live conversations, and much more. You now have all of the elements to your marketing foundation. It's your empowering tool to fill your prospect pipeline with loads of the kinds of clients you want.

Marketing is a fundamental skill for growing your business. As I've said, marketing is simply letting the clients that you most want to serve know that you exist. It's communicating what you are excellent at. Marketing is explaining what you do better than anyone else and what you love doing so you can be of service. And one more thing, it's attracting the right sorts of clients and letting them know that you're available to help them. The reason I beat this is drum so relentlessly is that as women, we often don't take care of our businesses or ourselves. Just like eating clean, whole food is fundamental to your health, attracting more of the right-fit clients is key to increasing your income. You have clients who need you, have emergencies, or just want you to hold their hand while they get through a problem or project. Too often women entrepreneurs place their clients' priorities ahead of the things they need to do to advance their businesses. You want to take care of your clients and at the same time have them respect your boundaries. Your family and your friends are, of course, important. And yet so is your business, because the more your business flourishes, the more you'll be able to support your family, do more of the things that you love, and help more clients.

My closing message to you is—empower yourself! Please put into action what I've taught you here about defining, knowing, and keeping your ideal client top of mind. And weed out non-ideal clients. Leverage the heck out of these exercises. Empower yourself with the clarity of knowing in such delicious detail more about the client you serve best compared to anyone else in your field. Never forget, few entrepreneurs invest the time and the deep thought required to get to know everything that matters to their ideal clients. But you're different! Or, you soon will be. You have this beautiful granite-strong, ocean-deep under-standing of the kinds of clients you want more of. Now use this!

The truth is, too many entrepreneurs fall victim to the so-called shiny object syndrome. They're easily distracted

by the latest apps for social media, whiz-bang photo editing, or productivity tracking. Don't get me wrong—social
media and productivity are important to growing your
business. I'd hate for you to lose sight of the firm foundation you've just built to attract more of the clients you
want to serve.

Marketing your business—whether you do it yourself,
hire a team member, or outsource parts of it to assistants
and contractors—is crucial to your success. However
you choose to market your business, you want to own
your ideal client and your marketing. The insights you've
gained by taking this deep dive into knowing your ideal
client and learning to speak their language are incredi-
bly valuable, and you've only just begun. So please take
the work you've accomplished with these exercises and
organize it into a binder or a file on your computer so that
you can use it often. I promise you that you'll make phe-
nomenally strong, wise, and profitable decisions for your
business and your ideal clients—as long as you keep your
ideal clients in mind. When you keep ideal clients in the
center of your mental dashboard you'll create exciting
programs they can't resist, irresistible content they can't
wait to gobble up, and they'll ask, "How do I work with
you?"

Why I Work with Women Entrepreneurs

They say change happens in an instant. For me it was
a pile of instants. As I said at the opening of this book,
I'm inspired every day by the amazing entrepreneurs I
have the honor of working with. In 2015, I began to see a

troubling pattern. I would work with entrepreneurs who were starting businesses, launching much-needed products and services, or stepping up their customer outreach. We'd implement a successful campaign, promotion, or launch. I diligently tried to keep the entrepreneur and her team involved as I developed messaging, blogs, articles, campaigns, and content plans—the building blocks of successful marketing. My hope was that they could learn the approaches and techniques. The problem I found was that I was the marketing consultant. Therefore, everybody else on the team had his or her own job to do and wasn't able to learn how to put the marketing programs into action. As much as I wished that they could learn from the strategies, tactics, and tools we implemented, when I finished a project, there was virtually no follow-through. That was endlessly frustrating for me.

Disturbing facts about the state of women-owned businesses began to gnaw at me. As a voracious researcher, I track statistics about the earning power of women entrepreneurs compared to our male counterparts. We could hope the well-documented fact that women earn less than men would be limited to corporate America. Sadly, that's not the case. There's an even wider earnings gap between women entrepreneurs and men entrepreneurs, according to the SBA in 2017.

FACT:
Women own 36 percent of all businesses in the US, and yet their sales amount to only 11 percent of total sales! Companies owned by men are just over half of all businesses, and their sales are a whopping 79 percent.

"This can't be!" I railed at my computer. After all, women become entrepreneurs to take charge of our own destiny. To earn incomes appropriate for the value we bring our clients. Don't we? I was disheartened.

I realized I had a bigger contribution to make. My mission now is to educate, prepare, and mentor women entrepreneurs who want to get a firm handle on the best ways to market to their ideal clients. Many women start businesses because they see problems that aren't being solved the way they know they can be. They said, "There's got to be a better way!" For example, women who struggled to find quality tutoring for their children decided to share their hard-earned knowledge and help moms searching for quality tutors and products. Or women who found that largely male financial advisors can be insensitive to the needs of a growing family, and others who saw people, families, and businesses struggling because no one offered the "better mousetrap" that women entrepreneurs knew was possible. The gap is: while many women have the better mousetrap, they don't understand that without an effective marketing plan and daily actions focused directly on reaching and educating their ideal clients, not enough clients will discover them.

It all came together for me this way: our community and our country have a lengthy list of problems that need to be solved. We need more women leading in all parts of our business, economy, culture, and society. Let's start with women business owners!

If this is you, take action! Implement the exercises in this book, choose your ideal, right-fit client, and follow the steps I've shared so you can get your message in front of more of them. The better job you do with marketing, the less selling you'll have to do because you'll attract more of the clients who have the kind of urgent needs that you are genius at helping them solve.

It's Time to Grow Your Business

My intention with this step-by-step program is to equip you to master your marketing mindset and build a savvy foundation for your important client attraction work. It's time for you to put your crystal-clear vision of the kinds of clients you want more of to work. It's time to be certain about who you want to work with so you can spark your prospects' interest, grow your business, and change the world—one amazing client at a time. I am sending you thousands of good thoughts and wishes for your success. You've got this!

After meeting so many talented women who are excellent at what they do, yet are not able to make the progress they want with their businesses because they weren't attracting enough of the right clients, I created the Client Clarity to Cash Flow System. This program is designed to help you get a firm handle on the person who is your ideal client, learn how to talk so they listen to you in content and conversations, and create an easy-to-implement structure for consistently attracting the right kinds of clients.

If you'd like more support to put your marketing foundation in place and grow your business so you can do the things you love, see the Contact Cynthia Page section of this book for three ways to work more closely with me.

You possess unique, hard-won skills, talents, and expertise. As I've said, do not forget there are clients out there who can learn best from you. They need your help. They're waiting for you. Our community, our economy, and indeed our planet, has weighty problems to solve. We need all of the purpose-driven women entrepreneurs like you we can get. Please get your message out so your clients can find you. I wish you success, fulfillment, and the business and life of your dreams.

About the Author

CYNTHIA TREVINO is a marketing expert and the cofounder of Resonnect Marketing, LLC. She's helped start-up founders, professionals, and business owners build awareness and recognition using social media, simplify their lives and bring in more clients, attraction marketing strategies and systems.

Cynthia Trevino worked for AT&T for over 20 years focusing on marketing. She also worked with technology startups in marketing and product management before becoming an entrepreneur. She has spent over 30 years helping businesses large and small attract customers, reach income goals, and fulfill missions. She earned a Bachelor's degree from San Diego State University in English Literature, and an MBA. from National University, also in San Diego. She honed her marketing expertise from hard-won experiences in the customer trenches.

Cynthia cofounded Resonnect Marketing, LLC, in 2001 with her partner and spouse, Jim Butz, in Carlsbad, California. She has guided business owners to the realization that if you're in business, you're in marketing. In the age of social media, you're also a content creator and publisher, and that's a wonderful way to start conversations with potential clients who don't know you yet.

Cynthia enjoys volunteering with organizations that empower women entrepreneurs to grow their businesses and make their communities, economy, and country stronger. She serves on the board of the San Diego Chapter of National Association of Women Business Owners (NAWBO).

Cynthia's mission is to ensure that every woman business owner on the planet knows her value, earns her worth, and makes the impact she is passionate about.

With her Client Clarity to Cash Flow Signature Program, Cynthia educates women business owners about how to understand their ideal clients better than anyone else and speak their language so they can attract more of them.

She lives in Carlsbad, California, with her husband. When she's not working with entrepreneurs looking to change the world (one amazing customer at a time), she enlists Jim and friends in the tasty search for the perfect pasta and Syrah pairing.

Contact Cynthia

You may have consumed every morsel of *She Markets, A Guide for Women Entrepreneurs: Five Simple Steps to Attract More Clients, Make More Money, and Have More Impact*, like a hungry college student devours a pizza. Yay for you! However, sometimes reading new, reshaped ideas and putting them into action are two totally different undertakings.

Did you create your perfect client description, pull language from client success stories, and create meaningful headlines so you can attract their attention?

Are you ready to begin speaking your clients' language in marketing, messaging, and conversations so you can make the impact you're here to make?

Have you prepared your **90-Day Client Connection Plan** to reach more ideal clients so you can do more of the work you love?

If you're feeling inspired to get started and overwhelmed about how to put all of this together, I'm so glad you're here!

Now is your time to invest in yourself and growing your business! Seize this moment to tap into your talents and everything you know about your best clients so you can reach more of them.

I've helped many entrepreneurs, just like you, master an understanding of their ideal clients, how to talk so they listen, and how to implement a simple structure for successful marketing. Clients say they didn't think they could "do this marketing thing" before taking my training. They like having the **Client Clarity to Cash Flow System** as a guide.

Many of us need help to get started with the right strategies. You can get help if you want to act now to attract more ideal clients so you can grow your business.

Are you...

- Tired of marketing—doing social media and networking with little to show for it?
- Frustrated by connecting with too many potential clients who waste your time?
- Struggling to figure out what to talk, blog, or post about on social media so you attract more clients who need you?
- Finding your business doesn't get the attention it deserves? Sick of hypey marketing that doesn't help you reach clients or grow your business?
- Overwhelmed by trying to do everything you think should in marketing, it isn't working, and you don't know what to try next?
- Uncertain of which strategies will be successful for your marketing, your business, and your dreams?
- Looking for a way to market your business so you don't feel salesy and still reach more ideal clients who help increase your income and your impact?

While we're excellent at our work, we're not all experts at everything required to grow our businesses. You may not have learned how to attract clients consistently. No one has taught you how to deeply understand your ideal client or organize content to make marketing easier. That's why I created the **Client Clarity to Cash Flow Signature Program.**

Here's exactly what you will get
when you work with me:

- Private, one-on-one training sessions
- The certainty of understanding the clients you want to serve so you can have more fun in your business
- Step-by-step lessons to build a marketing foundation for networking and content so you can have the income and effects you desire
- Discovering how to identify topics your clients care about for content, conversations, e-mails, blogs, headlines, and more
- Learning how to setup a marketing content plan so you can create the business of your dreams

Client Clarity To Cash Flow System

WEEK #1: Your New Magnetic Marketing Mindset
- Intention Setting for Your Client Clarity Program
- Magnetic Marketing Mindset lesson

WEEK #2: Meet Your Favorite, Ideal Client
- Lesson on how to know your perfect client better than anyone else

- Exercises to clarify, define, and deeply understand your ideal, profitable client

WEEK #3: Get a Firm Handle on Your Clients' Top Pain Points and Problems
- Lesson: paint a vivid picture of your clients' life/ business after working with you
- Exercises and questions to uncover what you know about their world

WEEK #4: Learn How to Speak Your Clients' Language in Marketing Messages
- Tools for communicating that you understand their pain points
- Brainstorming session to create content headlines

WEEK #5: Design Your 90-Day Client Connection Plan
- Choosing and organizing themes and headlines for your game plan

WEEK #6: Implementation
- Developing your formula for client attraction
- How to accomplish content creation, distribution, and sharing

How to contact me:

Website: **https://www.clientconversioncoach.com/**
LinkedIn: **https://www.linkedin.com/in/cynthiatrevino/**
Email: **cytrevino@resonnect.com**
Phone: **+1.760.268.1199**

Acknowledgments

They say none of us gets here alone. And I am no exception. I am grateful to so many people who helped me shape, mold, refine, and distill the knowledge and experiences that I poured into this book. **Pamela Hendrickson** is a marketing, content, and framework genius. Thank you for being an excellent trainer. Thanks to **Jeanne Hurlbert, PhD,** for incredible insights about understanding customers and your generosity. Thank you to **Lisa Sasevich** for the rich lessons and wonderful community. Thank you to **Lisa Cherney** for valuable knowledge and always sharing the perfect thought when I, or someone else, was stuck. Thank you **Shawn Marie Turi** for your guidance.

I am indebted to the entire team at **Author Bridge Media** for teaching me how to build a book. Thank you, **Helen Chang,** for sharing your knowledge and for our partnership. I'm so glad we met when we did. Thank you to **Katherine MacKenett,** a world-class editor. A thousand thanks for your consistently patient and valuable feedback and recommendations on the entire manuscript. I so appreciated the **San Diego Hera Hub** coworking community, founded by **Felena Hanson.** These women entrepreneurs consistently provide timely suggestions and ideas when I send out an S.O.S. Thanks to **Ariela Wilcox.** And heartfelt thanks to **Shelley Murasko, Teri King, Patricia Rundblade,** and **Billie Frances.**

Many thanks to **David Wogahn** for your expertise and hand holding for my book cover and design.

My late dad was the first feminist I ever knew. He taught me from the age of 7 that if I did well in school, and graduated from college, I could be independent. While this concept is a given today, it was far from the case when I grew up in the 1950s. I miss him every day and am eternally grateful for his guidance.

Finally, eternal gratitude to **Jim Butz,** my husband, for his unwavering patience, deep belief in me, and endless support. I love you to Mars and back.